Social Work & ICT

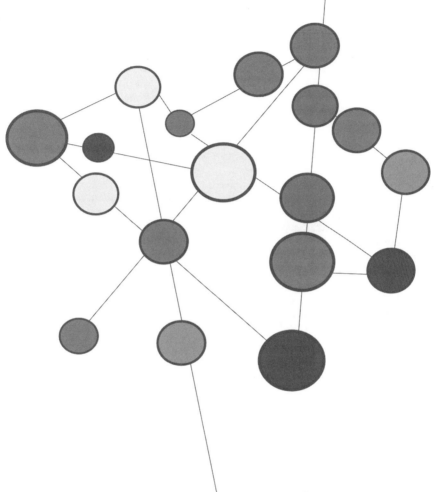

Andrew Hill & Ian Shaw

SAGE

Los Angeles | London | New Delhi
Singapore | Washington DC

First published 2011

SAGE Publications Ltd
1 Oliver's Yard
55 City Road
London EC1Y 1SP

SAGE Publications Inc.
2455 Teller Road
Thousand Oaks, California 91320

SAGE Publications India Pvt Ltd
B 1/I 1 Mohan Cooperative Industrial Area
Mathura Road
New Delhi 110 044

SAGE Publications Asia-Pacific Pte Ltd
33 Pekin Street #02-01
Far East Square
Singapore 048763

Library of Congress Control Number: 2010934860

British Library Cataloguing in Publication data

A catalogue record for this book is available from the British Library

ISBN 978-1-84920-055-4
ISBN 978-1-84920-056-1 (pbk)

Typeset by C&M Digitals (P) Ltd, Chennai, India
Printed by CPI Antony Rowe, Chippenham, Wiltshire
Printed on paper from sustainable resources

MIX
Paper from
responsible sources
FSC   www.fsc.org   FSC® C013604

Contents

About the Authors

Andrew Hill is Director of the MA in Social Work Programme in the Department of Social Policy and Social Work at the University of York, England, and Lecturer in Social Work. He is a qualified social worker with a background in social work with children and families, including family support and child protection, fostering and adoption, and working therapeutically with abused children and young people. He has researched and written about play therapy for sexually abused children and the role of non-abusing carers. He is author of *Working in Statutory Contexts*, in which he examines the skills required for statutory social work and how such work may be consistent with anti-oppressive practice.

Ian Shaw is Director of the Graduate School in the Department of Social Policy and Social Work at the University of York, England, and Professor of Social Work. He co-founded the journal *Qualitative Social Work*, and initiated the European Conference for Social Work Research. Much of his work is on the borders and research and practice, and sociology and social work, and is often informed by an interest in qualitative methodology. His recent work includes the *Sage Handbook of Social Work Research*. His current research includes the historical relationship between social work and sociology, especially in the USA. His forthcoming book is a reworking of his *Evaluating in Practice*.

Introduction

It has become commonplace to talk of 'the IT revolution', and to compare it with the industrial revolution of the eighteenth and nineteenth centuries – so rapid, so widespread and so profound have been the changes brought about by recent advances in information and communication technologies (ICTs). It seems that, in a very short space of time, computer-enabled communication and information storage has become an integral part not only of many people's working lives, but also of the fabric of their social lives and their leisure activities. Increasingly we work, shop, play and socialise online.

Given that social work is, according to the UK Department of Health's careers website, 'all about people' (Department of Health, 2007) it should not be surprising that ICTs have also become a highly significant part of social work. New, electronic communication methods are being used by professionals and service users alike, both formally and informally. New methods for storing and sharing information about people and about the complexity of their daily lives and circumstances are being introduced rapidly across social work.

This book seeks to assess the extent and the nature of the changes that are happening in social work, and to ask how they relate to the notion of 'best practice'. The book is about the *relationship* between good social work practice and information and communication technologies (ICTs). The small word 'and' in the title is therefore highly significant. The book considers how the increasing integration of ICTs may be changing the face of social work, for good or ill, and also how social work may perhaps be shaping the development and the use of ICTs. We do not assume that the relationship between ICT and social work is necessarily a case of one-way traffic – new ideas from the world of ICT leading to new forms of social work practice. It may be that existing social work practices lead to changes in the way in which ICTs are understood, configured and utilised. But we are social work academics, not ICT specialists, and our primary concern is to promote critical thinking about what constitutes best practice in social work when it comes to its relationship with ICTs, whether that is at the individual level of social workers and service users or at the level of the organisations that employ or represent them. We set out some ideas about best practice in Chapter 1.

Some may think that ICTs and social work are rather strange bedfellows. ICTs may have a seemingly all-pervasive reach into every area of our lives – but are they really suitable for social work? After all, social work and computers seem to have very different logics. Computers are usually perceived to be all about standardised, unemotional processing of information, whereas social work is about paying attention to the needs and feelings of individual human beings. Computers are about speed and efficiency, whereas good social work practice goes at the pace of the individual service user. Computers, so it is thought, are best at doing sums and reaching quantitative, statistical judgements, whereas social work is largely about gathering and analysing qualitative information and making complex, situated, professional judgements. In fact, throughout the book we will be challenging the different strands of this apparent mismatch. We suggest that the relationship between social work and ICT may be rather more complex than the above sketch suggests and that, where there are tensions, they may not be the ones listed above.

What is for certain is that ICTs are already an integral part of contemporary social work, and we can safely say that in the future they are very likely to become further embedded in practice. For example, computer-assisted communication tools are of great benefit to people with certain types of disabilities (Murray and Aspinall, 2006). And online information, support and counselling services for young people are becoming increasingly mainstream, even in statutory agencies such as the Children and Families Courts Advisory and Support Service (Cafcass, 2010), because of the perceived benefits of convenience, flexibility, and the degree of user control. ICTs are being used to support learning amongst social workers, both on qualifying courses and afterwards, in social work agencies. But there are also serious concerns about social work and ICTs. For example, GPS tracking is being used with offenders in ways that have raised significant objections from the outset about the erosion of civil liberties, and the role that social workers may have in that process (Nellis, 1991). Complex electronic databases are being used for record keeping and assessment in work with children and families in ways that have raised concerns about the amount of time social workers must now spend in front of the computer, rather than with service users (Social Work Taskforce, 2009b).

ICT is already a part of the fabric of social work, and there is every indication that it is here to stay. There are advantages and disadvantages, opportunities and threats associated with this. If our concern is to promote best social work practice then our task must be to work out how to maximise the advantages, and minimise the disadvantages that are associated with ICTs in social work. This is fundamentally the approach we have taken throughout this book. But before we can begin this task, there are two deeper questions that we should first consider.

Assessing Social Work and ICT

As we have seen, ICTs may be here 'for good or ill' – but how do we decide what is 'good' and what is 'ill'? Some of the examples given above are relatively straightforward. It is quite difficult to see any significant disadvantages for disabled people in using computer technology to communicate with others if impairment means that they are otherwise unable to do so. Yet other examples are far from clear cut. How do we assess the relative advantages and disadvantages of complex electronic databases for record keeping and assessment work with children and families? Proponents claim that they have significant advantages. If, as claimed, such databases can help with quality control processes, and if they can facilitate information sharing, then does this offset the cost that we noted earlier of using increasing amounts of social worker time for 'data input' and, if so, by how much?

One way of approaching these questions is to separate out the different interests of all those involved. It seems clear that social work managers have a primary interest in 'quality control' processes, although service users and social workers also have an interest in good quality standards. But, in introducing ICTs, managers may also be responding to a government e-agenda that includes financial targets for local authorities, and these financial goals may not be shared by service users and social workers. In Chapter 3 we include some other examples of social work and ICT in which the interests of service users, social workers and their managers do not coincide.

But, of course, separating out the differing perspectives and interests is just an analytical device. It doesn't tell us whose interests we should consider to be the most important. That question demands that we pay attention to the ethics and values that we hold, and it takes us into the world of social and moral philosophy. In this respect, O'Donnell and Henriksen (2002) give a helpful account of the philosophical foundations for an evaluation of the social impact of ICT. Their work is about the social impact of ICT as a whole, and not just in relation to social work. O'Donnell and Henriksen suggest that 'technological, largely market-orientated, functionalist and instrumental worldviews dominate ICT discourse' (2002: 89). They contrast this with 'the critical neo-humanist perspective of emancipation and human potential' that they argue can form the basis for a valid evaluation of the social impact of ICT: one that pays attention to the 'lifeworld' and to the interest of citizens, rather than to the interest of those with money and power.

For us, as social work academics, this seems a familiar line of argument. Our approach here is to assess social work and ICT in the light of the aims, values and ethics of social work as a profession – not in the light of the values that may dominate the discourse about ICT. Later in the book we draw on codes of social work ethics produced in the UK by the British Association of Social Workers (BASW, 2002) and in the USA by the National Association of Social Workers (NASW, 2008). We acknowledge that this approach does not completely reconcile the sometimes competing interests of service users, managers and agencies that we identified earlier – and the codes of ethics themselves recognise this, at least implicitly. The aims and values of social work are not uncontested. But it does provide us with a clear position for assessing ICT and social work – one that understands that practice developments involving ICT should be assessed in the light of the aims, values and ethics of social work, in the same way as any other practice development.

Responding to Social Work and ICT

But there is a second question to consider before we can move on to our central task of working out how to maximise the advantages and minimise the disadvantages of integrating ICTs into social work practice. The way we have framed the task suggests that social work that includes the use of ICTs is a kind of practice that we can shape and mould for particular ends. But this is not the only way of looking at it.

Some might argue that the colonisation of social work by ICTs is an inevitable process that is very difficult to resist or change. There are a number of powerful structural drivers. Statutory agencies in the UK are responding to government policy that is moving rapidly towards online delivery of the full range of public services. For example, at the time of writing, Gordon Brown, then UK Prime Minister, had just announced the creation of new website, MyGov to replace the current DirectGov. This new 'dashboard' site will hold personal details and

> will end the current frustration of web users needing to identify themselves separately for different public services. [Gordon Brown] also said the dashboard will allow the citizen to manage their pensions, tax credits and child benefits, as well as pay council tax, fix doctors or hospital appointments, apply for schools of their choice and communicate with children's teachers. (Wintour, 2010)

By the time you read this text no doubt things will have moved on considerably. We will have more to say in Chapter 3 about how this policy objective of online public service delivery affects social work in particular. Another of the drivers pushing ICT into social work is the understanding that individual welfare agencies need to work closely together (not only, but perhaps most urgently, as a result of inquiries into child deaths). Families may experience multiple forms of oppression arising perhaps from mental ill health, disability or poverty, and they may be receiving help from a range of specialist social workers, other professionals, volunteers and peers. In a previous generation, the solution to this was the creation, in 1971, of social services departments in which individual social workers had generic skills and were able to work with the whole range of issues (see Seebohm, 1968). Nowadays the preferred solution is to make the records of each professional involvement easily available in electronic format to all the others involved, by using ICTs. Of course, this places a new (and, in some circumstances, perhaps unhelpful) emphasis on full, timely and accurate recording. Then there is the more general driver of what we might call 'cultural expectation' in the use of ICTs. These days, social workers do not expect to have to search filing cabinets of paper files by hand for access to basic information about the social work services being provided to service users. As we will see in Chapter 5, even social workers who are sceptical about a particular record keeping system (the ICS) understand the power and utility of computer-held records and are broadly in favour of developing functional systems. And service users have the expectation that, as with the best consumer-orientated organisations, when they contact social work agencies the details of their previous contacts will be available to the relevant professional via a quick computer search so that they do not have to repeat information.

In the book we shall certainly present evidence to suggest that, in some circumstances, social workers experience ICTs as being imposed on them. Some feel that it is being forced into their practice in ways that they find inappropriate. Yet there is also evidence to suggest that social workers find ways of resisting such impositions, and that they find ways of ameliorating what they see as the negative effects. More positively there is evidence of service users and social workers alike embracing the new technologies enthusiastically and using them to further aims that fit with the central values of social work.

So the debate about the ways in which we can respond to the growing incorporation of ICT into social work practice is complex. We do not want to argue that we are free to develop best practice in social work and ICT in any direction we like, without regard to the various structural forces that are driving the ever increasing integration of ICTs. But on the other hand we do not want to argue that those forces represent the whole story. Power relationships at the local level are likely to be very significant in shaping the way in which social work relates to ICTs in any specific context. These power relationships include (but are not restricted to) those between managers, social workers and service users that we referred to earlier. We will develop these arguments more fully in the next chapter as we present ideas about best practice and strategies for achieving it.

The Structure of the Book

The book starts with a chapter that contains our ideas about the possible shape of best social work practice with ICTs. In many ways this first chapter is at the heart of the book. The chapter is designed to stand alone, but some of the evidence that we draw on is to be found later in the book.

The second chapter is an initial survey of the different functional components of social work practice (from advertising available services, through referral processes, to assessments, interventions and review and evaluation). The chapter reports on current developments and shows how ICTs have become an integral part of each component. At the same time it considers the reasons for the integration of ICT in the components of practice and looks at the claims made by the proponents of ICTs.

Chapters 3 to 5 contain a more critical account of the ways in which the practices of social work relate to the use of ICTs. Here we look at evidence relating to the 'impact' of ICTs on social work, both positive and negative, from the perspectives of services users (Chapter 3), social workers (Chapter 4) and social work agencies (Chapter 5). We will have more to say in Chapter 3 about how we understand the term 'impact'.

As social work educators we are interested not only in social work practice, but also in the process of learning and teaching in social work. ICTs are being increasingly woven into the fabric of teaching and learning. In Chapters 6 and 7 we consider the impact of ICTs within educational institutions during qualifying or post-qualifying education (Chapter 6) and in practice settings at any stage in a social work career (Chapter 7).

Chapters 3 to 5 on social work practice, and Chapters 6 and 7 on teaching learning in social work, contain material that forms the basis for the ideas in Chapter 1, about best social work practice and ICTs.

Each chapter ends with a section headed 'Taking it Further'. We regard these as a central part of the book, rather than an optional add-on for those so minded to give them a go. They include suggestions for further reading, websites to visit, and a variety of tasks and exercises that can be done individually or in groups. An aside will help. We find it helpful to distinguish three sorts of knowledge: theoretical knowledge ('knowing that'), craft or skill knowledge ('knowing how'), and practical-moral knowledge ('knowing from'). Within this context, the 'Taking it Further' end sections are pitched to achieve two general aims. First, for a text that is about forms of practice, it is essential but not sufficient to acquire knowledge only as 'knowing that'. ICT knowledge will also be a practical or applied knowledge. But when we talk about 'application', something more is intended than the instrumental sense of practicality; by 'application' we mean the more fundamental sense of making something relevant to oneself. This involves a particular kind of knowledge – 'knowing from within or practical-moral knowledge', which 'requires not cleverness in application but understanding' (Schwandt, 1997: 76). 'Practical-moral knowledge aims to actually move people, not simply give them good ideas' (p. 81). Second, 'Taking it Further' indicates that we see these sections as supporting readers in pushing ahead from the basis provided in this book.

We have pursued a balancing act throughout this book. On the one hand, our primary aim has been to write in a way that takes the reader beyond the first generation 'How to cope with IT' books, and to challenge readers to ask why ICT is used and how this affects and impacts on practice and the experience of people who use services. At the same time, as explained a moment ago, we have sought to facilitate a practical knowledge. This means that you will come across numerous URL addresses. While most of these have endured for some years at the time of writing, some will inevitably disappear. When that happens we hope you will sense the general reference we are making, and will be able to pursue the application elsewhere.

1

Best Practice for Social Work and ICT

In this chapter we make a set of suggestions as to how ICTs may be used to further the aims of social work in ways that accord with the values of the profession. Some of these suggestions are based on research findings that are discussed more fully later in the book, whilst other suggestions are, we acknowledge, rather more tentative in nature. We give some indication as to which is which.

Our ideas are framed as being about best practice in social work. The concept of 'best practice' is widely used in healthcare, as well as in business management and in the world of ICTs, to mean the most efficient and effective way of doing things: ways that use the minimum resources and yet give the optimum results. There is a danger that it can become quite a utilitarian concept. In the context of professional social work, often there are inbuilt tensions between the drive for efficiency and the need, for example, to respect the individuality of service users and to work at their pace. In their exploration of the concept of 'best practice' in social work Jones and colleagues argue that we must take into account the complexity and the difficulty of social work tasks where there are

> no straightforward actions which could protect or promote the welfare of one person or group without possibly causing distress or even deeply hurting and restricting theirs and other's rights and freedoms. (Jones et al., 2008: 3)

In this book we follow Jones and colleagues' argument that best practice in social work must fit with a critical stance, and, as we remarked above, with the core aims and values of the profession. Best practice does not mean that the process or outcomes are perfect, nor that there are no constraints on what can be accomplished, but it should indicate the best that could be achieved in a specific situation, with a specific set of people and circumstances. This book seeks to develop an understanding of best practice in social work that includes the use of ICTs.

The current chapter is divided into three sections. The first discusses overarching principles that may help to define features of best practice with social work and ICTs. The second focuses in on elements of best practice in service delivery, and the final section is about best practice in professional training and ongoing professional development of social workers.

General Principles of Best Practice

A practice-led approach

One of the commonest ways of thinking about ICTs is to regard them as tools that can be used for a variety of jobs. As new ICT tools are developed, so they are applied to existing tasks in ways that may enable them to be done more quickly, or more efficiently. But in applying ICTs in order to gain the benefits, it is often the case that the tasks themselves are changed in significant ways, regardless of whether or not any improvement is achieved.

One of us drafted this chapter. So, for example, in producing this text I am using an electronic word processor. In my case this is only marginally faster than the much older method of using pen and paper, but it has many additional benefits. The software corrects my spelling and grammar as I write, it keeps count of how many words I have written, and it enables me to send the text quickly and easily to my co-author for comment. But using a word processor has also changed the process of my writing in subtle ways. It means that I can experiment with ideas more freely, in the knowledge that I can move sentences around easily without the laborious process of having to cross out and rewrite. But it means that probably I waste more time on 'polishing' text, because there is no longer the need to concentrate on getting it right the first time. Word processors came into general use in the 1980s, and began to be more widely used in universities in the 1990s, so the example is dated. But new technologies continue to evolve, and a common pattern continues to be that, as they are developed, so new ways are found of using them to do existing tasks, and old ways of doing things are modified.

Social work has not been immune to this process. There is a tendency to see a new development in the field of ICTs, and possibly its application elsewhere in business, commerce or industry, and to ask how the advantages of this new technology can be brought to social work. This can be thought of as a technology-led approach. It is not without merit, but there are significant dangers. In this book we argue for an approach to ICT that is practice-led and that puts social work first.

One of the dangers of a technology-led approach is that social work comes to be understood primarily in the light of the aims of ICT developers, and evaluated in their terms. For example, recent advances in networking mean that it no longer makes sense for workers in large social work organisations to store information on the hard drives of individual computers. Common practice is to use a central filestore that can be accessed by any authorised user from any computer on the network (or sometimes over the internet). This means that there are reliable systems for data backup, and it allows rapid sharing of information. But it means that social workers no longer need their own office computer – any will do – so that the sharing of computer terminals (often called hot-desking), and mobile and home working have become widespread. This makes sense from an ICT perspective, but what of the changes to social work practice? We know that social work is stressful work that has a significant emotional content (Howe, 2008). Working face to face with service users who may be distressed, angry or otherwise disturbing in their presentation means that the emotional and other support of colleagues is, for social workers, an essential ingredient in their practice. It may be that flexible, ICT-led patterns of working undermine the cohesiveness of teams of practitioners who meet each other less frequently and less predictably. So the use of networked filestores should not be understood and evaluated from an ICT perspective alone. We need a practice-led approach that takes into account the practice perspective and, in this case, draws attention to potential disadvantages.

In this example, and more generally, best practice means a practice-led approach to the use of ICTs. We have contrasted this with a technology-led approach, but it should be acknowledged that some elements of the latter approach coincide quite closely with what we might think of as management interests in social work. For example, the introduction of central filestores fits with the management goal of increased efficiency. This complicates the argument, because we do not wish to argue for inefficient organisations – there is no benefit in that to anyone. Instead we should recognise that the concept of social work practice itself contains a complex blend of the sometimes complementary and sometimes competing interests of service users, social workers and managers. Our argument (that best practice in social work and ICT means a practice-led approach) does not exclude the interests of social work managers. More positively, adopting best practice and a practice-led approach means starting with social work practice, not with the ICTs themselves.

It is important to make a distinction within the term 'practice-led'. For much of the book we have in mind 'social work practice' when we use the term 'practice-led'. But we intend a broader meaning of the word practice. The practice of social workers, for example, is not the same as the practice of social work educators or even social work students. So when we come to Chapters 6 and 7, the agenda we address is led by the practice of learning, and by implication, the practice of facilitating that learning. The same widening of the distinction also applies when we consider aspects of ICT and service users. In Chapter 3 we give some illustrations of how the perspectives of professionals and service users part company regarding technology. Towards the end of that chapter we pose the challenging questions that arise when we suggest that it makes good, if provocative, sense to talk in terms of service user, carer and citizen-led ICT interests. Each of these discussions will caution against assuming that 'practice-led' will always mean 'social work practitioner led'. But it will always be set against 'technology-led'.

This is one reason why throughout the book we seek to understand particular contexts for social work and to ask which technologies are being used and why, and to understand how practice may be changing as a result. Best practice means that our assessment of those changes draws on the aims and values of social work as a whole.

Best practice in shaping an ICT infrastructure

Another of the dangers of a technology-led approach is the tendency in social work for purpose-built ICT systems to be experienced by those using them as profoundly user-unfriendly. In Chapter 4 we will consider a number of examples in some detail, but suffice to say that there is significant research and other evidence to show that social workers have found the introduction of electronic ways of recording and processing their day to day work to be at best distracting, and at worst frustrating and deeply unhelpful. One of the features of social workers' critique is that the design and implementation of such systems is being imposed on them by people who don't fully understand the job. ICT developers and the social work managers who commission and buy the products, so the argument goes, do not have sufficient understanding of the day to day realities of social work practice to come up with useful systems.

In fact, the literature about best practice in the design and development of ICT systems for organisations has long recognised this problem. Some have called for an ethnographic approach to ICT systems design: one that starts with ICT developers spending time within an organisation so as to gain detailed information about its working practices before starting work on ICT systems (for example Heath and Luff, 2000). But this approach does not entirely solve the problem. It continues to exclude users from the design process, and it is almost impossible to foresee all the implications of a new system by studying only the work practices that exist before it is introduced. Hartswood and colleagues (2002) argue for a process of 'co-realisation', by which they mean that ICT professionals and the 'users' of ICT systems should together create, implement, and continue to develop ICT systems. They suggest that the ICT professionals need to move beyond a narrow 'engineering' mentality and physically move to work for long periods within the organisation, not just in the design phase but, crucially, in the subsequent implementation phase. It is in this latter phase, when people actually start to make use of a system for the first time, that there is the most opportunity for users to shape both their own ICT-enabled practice and the development of the system. Yet most of the social work users of the ICT systems we will consider in this book had no contact with ICT professionals in the design phase, let alone during implementation.

If ICT professionals need to become immersed in the world and work of social work ICT users, then social workers, in turn, need to become more skilled in understanding and using ICT. Hartswood and colleagues argue that this happens naturally as a by-product of the co-realisation process that they envisage, particularly during the implementation phase, as users gain experience of the system.

> As users become 'experienced' they develop new ways of using the system that in turn generate new ideas for its further development. Rather than users simply adapting themselves to the new system, co-realisation stresses a change not only in the user, but also in their use of the system as a set of working practices evolve through use. Furthermore, we would argue that through this process users gain more general IT competences and become better able to judge *inter alia* what is possible and what is not, what is simple and what takes time. (Hartswood et al., 2002: 24)

During the period we were writing this book, criticism of one UK government-led ICT system in social work, the Integrated Children's System (see Chapters 3 and 4), led to a review and to a commitment to allow continuing local development, in line with local needs. What is still missing from policy is a commitment to bring ICT professionals and social work users of ICT closer together in a long term engagement. Such a development has the potential to lead to ICT systems that are configured by best social work practices and 'owned' by social workers, rather than continuing to have social work practice configured to meet the needs of ICT systems.

Service users and ICT infrastructure

The discussion so far about working together on creating ICT infrastructure for social work has been about the relationship between ICT professionals and social workers. Yet in recent years social work has begun to understand the value of listening to what service users have to say – not just about their own situations, but about wider issues in the shaping and delivery of social work services. Crucially, the organisation in England and Wales that is dedicated to supporting best practice in social work, the Social Care Institute for Excellence (SCIE), argues that there is a central role in its work for people who use services (Social Care Institute for Excellence, 2010). Yet we should acknowledge that developing such a role is a complex task, not least because a significant proportion of 'users' of statutory services are 'involuntary' (up to a third in some studies) (Ferguson, 2005) and that special skills may be required for working in statutory contexts where 'service users' may resist attempts to control their behaviour and to get them to change (Hill, 2010).

So, given the current lack of involvement of social workers, and the complexity of involving service users, is it sensible to suggest that best practice in the design of social work ICT infrastructure should include both groups? The key argument is that the 'data' under discussion is directly or indirectly about service users and, despite the complex dynamics of statutory settings, service users have rights not only to access their data but also to have a say in how it is created, managed and shared with others. In our view there is an opportunity here to extend the kind of best practice with service users that has been championed by SCIE into the vexed area of ICT infrastructure.

Consent, confidentiality, privacy and data security

The increasing use of ICTs in social work raises some new questions in relation to consent, confidentiality, privacy and data security. However, in considering them we should be led by the relevant, local legal requirements and by the values and ethics of the profession, rather than by the logic of the ICTs themselves. Social workers have codes of ethics (for the

UK see BASW, 2002; for the US see NASW, 2008); and internationally see IFSW, 2005). Whilst these codes do not specifically highlight the use of ICTs, nonetheless we argue in Chapter 3 that these ethical principles should be used to guide best practice in the new contexts brought about by new uses of ICTs. In the US, the National Association of Social Workers has issued *Standards for Technology and Social Work Practice* (NASW, 2005) and we draw on that helpful document in what follows.

Best practice means that consent to a social work intervention which involves the use of ICT is required unless the service user lacks the capacity to give it, or the intervention has a legal mandate that overrides their wishes. This means that full information about data collection, storage and sharing systems should be provided for all service users as a part of giving information about the social work service. Most work will be carried out on the basis of informed consent, including consent to the use of ICT systems, but the choices of some 'involuntary' service users may be restricted by the legal mandate.

Various ethical dilemmas become apparent as we try to define the limits of confidentiality in modern social work. The primary right of service users to privacy means that securing the confidentiality of personal records remains the formal default position in all legal jurisdictions that we are aware of. But the operational need to share information with other agencies so as to provide a high-quality, coordinated service for service users, and the need to protect vulnerable people and, sometimes, the public as a whole, means that there is increasing pressure in the other direction. The use of ICTs has made it much easier to share information quickly and has, arguably, added to the assumption that data will be shared. We give the example of ContactPoint in Chapter 5. But best practice means not being driven to share information simply by the ICT-enabled ability to do so. The advent of email, for example, has probably led to more widespread inappropriate – and inadvertent – data sharing. Of course, it may be entirely appropriate to share information about a service user with another agency for the reasons given above. But best practice should continue to have regard to the legal and ethical framework for such decisions.

Concerns about data security have increased greatly with the growing use of ICT and with reported, high-profile losses of UK government data (Sweney, 2009). Once again, best practice means that, at an individual level, social workers must comply with the relevant law and with agency proce- dure for data handling. For example, the Youth Justice Board lists the 'dos' and 'don'ts' of data security in a leaflet for staff (Youth Justice Board, 2008). This includes detailed practical advice about the encryption of data on laptops, memory sticks, and so on. Best practice at the organisational level means that ICT systems must be designed with data security in mind. However, there is a trade-off between data security and ease of access, and some developments in social work ICT raise serious questions about the impact on civil liberties, as we will see in relation to ContactPoint in Chapter 5.

Access to ICT

Social work services and systems that are based on the use of ICTs must necessarily exclude those who do not have access to them. There may be many 'digital divides' (Norris, 2001) between and within countries in relation to access to ICTs that broadly match other well established inequalities, for example in relation to income, health and so on. But there is no simple correlation between digital divides and other forms of social exclusion, as evidenced, for example, by the effective use of online campaigning by disabled people that we refer to in Chapter 3. Following from social work's commitment to social justice, best practice means that social workers should be active in seeking to understand and to overcome digital divides. Insofar as social work services are advertised or delivered online, best practice means that we should seek to maximise accessibility, including for disabled people.

Appropriate engagement with service-user-led ICT

The discussion so far of the general features of good practice in social work and ICTs has been about the activities of professionals. But it is important to understand that service users are also making extensive use of ICTs, both independently and in conjunction with professional groups, and that this is a growing trend. We review some of this activity in Chapter 3. Now clearly it does not make much sense to suggest features of best practice in relation to the independent activities of service users, since the concept of best practice arises in professional contexts. But we suggest that social workers need to engage, for example, with websites set up and run by service users. Sometimes these may be critical of professional services and, depending on the nature of the critique, engagement may lead to service development. On other occasions, engagement may lead to joint action, for example in relation to service user participation in social work education. Social workers need to be aware of and to engage with the ways in which service users are making use of new technologies to communicate their experiences of social work services.

Best Practice in Delivering Social Work Services

Online service delivery

At the time of writing, few social work services in the UK are delivered entirely online, for reasons that we discuss in Chapter 4. The area in which there has been most growth has been the development of online counselling services, either in real time or asynchronous, where there may be a number of advantages to service users arising from the potential anonymity that it may provide. There is a UK Association for Counselling and Therapy Online (acto), with its own code of ethics (acto, 2010). This online counselling approach has been extended into mainstream social work with young people, with the NSPCC and Cafcass offering online support, including peer mentoring, to young service users.

The potential for misrepresentation (by professionals or by service users) means that best practice is for professionals to identify themselves clearly and accurately, and to take reasonable steps to verify the identity and contact information of service users. Websites should provide full details of professional name, qualifications, office address, contact details and links to appropriate regulatory or licensing bodies. In addition, those offering services online need to ensure the integrity and security of the computer systems they are using and to make arrangements to cover the possibility of server outage or breakdown. But these elements of best practice deal with what might be thought of as 'technical' issues. Of interest throughout this book are the ways in which technology mediates practice, and vice versa. So it is interesting to note that, according to acto, counsellors should 'be aware of and familiarize themselves with the differences between online and face to face psychological therapy and the impact that online work can have on the relationship between therapist and client and the therapeutic process' (2010). At the time of writing there appears to be some evidence in relation to outcomes (e.g., Murphy et al., 2009) but less to guide therapists in relation to the differences in process.

Online assessment tools

Whilst online service delivery might still be fairly unusual, many local authorities are developing ways in which members of the public can at least check their entitlement to community care services by completing online assessment forms, even if this is followed by a face to face assessment by a social worker. In some authorities the aim is to carry out the assessments entirely online, though the resulting support services are necessarily delivered face to face.

The rationing of such services through the creation of eligibility criteria is, of course, a contentious area of social work. So it seems to us that best practice in the development of online assessments should pay attention to the issues raised by the concept of a 'digital divide' (see Chapter 3) and should include openness about the eligibility criteria, and about the basis on which decisions are made.

Best practice in electronic recording and assessment protocols

The influence of electronic recording and assessment protocols on social work practice is discussed in Chapters 4 and 5. It seems that this is an area in which the relationship between technology and practice is vexed. We report on recent studies that demonstrate that, whilst social workers see many advantages in using up to date technology to record their work, nonetheless they report serious misgivings about systems currently in use. These ideas about the features of best practice take into account those concerns.

First, as we have already argued, best practice means that social workers should play a full role, alongside ICT specialists, in developing ICT infra-structure. Second, recording systems should allow social workers to 'tell the story' of their work with service users in ways that make narrative sense. Social workers are often critical of the ways in which current sys-tems force them to record different pieces of 'information' about service users in different computerised 'fields' in ways that make it difficult to understand the whole picture. At the very least, we need ICT approaches that are geared to handling larger sections of text – perhaps in the manner of e-books. Third, computerised recording systems should be easy to use and not get in the way of face to face work. We need to pay attention to the ways in which recording systems may influence the relationships between social workers and service users and design systems that support productive working relationships. Finally, we need to develop clear rules about privacy and data sharing that do not assume that personal informa-tion should be shared with other agencies simply because the technology exists to do so. Service users should continue to have control over their own data, even if there are some statutory contexts in which information may be shared with other agencies without the explicit consent of the person con-cerned. This is a difficult area in which law and policy are evolving rapidly.

Best Practice in Social Work Education and Ongoing Professional Development

Social work education

As we observe in Chapter 6, each new cohort of social work students has an increasing ease and familiarity with ICTs, both for study and for social-ising. This new world of electronic social networks is the background against which developments in e-learning are taking place. Nonetheless, it is not necessarily the case that all students will have developed the specific technical skills required for making formal use of the burgeoning number of electronic resources that are available to them. Best practice in the use of ICTs in education means ensuring that students become familiar with the wide range of relevant electronic resources – many of which are dis-cussed in Chapter 6 – and that they are equipped with the appropriate search skills.

At its best, the incorporation of Web 2.0 technologies into learning and teaching offers the opportunity to increase the amount of participation and interaction in learning. It allows, for example, for online group support for students on placement in geographically dispersed settings. It allows for connections with service users and other students in places and at times that would otherwise be impossible. But the ephemeral nature of Web 'knowledge' poses serious problems and means that best practice in e-learning must place an emphasis on critical thinking about information sources.

Professional development

As with social work education, ICTs open up access for social workers to a whole range of new online resources of varying types. Best social work practice demands a commitment to making use of these new resources and to developing a critical approach to the 'knowledge' contained therein. But ICTs also open up access to social learning networks, meaning that social workers can learn from and with people other than those in their geo-graphical workplace. In Chapter 7 we note that such networks are often used not only for substantive learning in relation to specific topics, but also for the kind of peer support and encouragement that operates at a more emotional level. This may be surprising given the association between computerisation and 'remoteness' or lack of feelings, but the evidence sug-gests that people are adept at communicating feelings through text. Best practice should recognise the validity of learning networks in relation to both substantive learning about a topic and peer support. In Chapter 7 we consider 'communities of practice' – one way in which this is being developed – and we suggest that these may have a significant role to play.

Taking it further

This paired exercise will be especially helpful at the commencement of a practice placement, or on newly taking up a practice post.

1 Find out what the agency policy is for data security and consent and obtain the evidence for this.
2 Identify the various points at which decisions about data access have been embedded in agency policy documents. What accessibility issues and potential digital divides does your assessment raise and reveal?

2

ICT Use in Social Work

This chapter considers how and why a whole range of ICTs are currently being used within social work. In Chapter 1 we argued for the importance of an approach that is led by practice considerations rather than by the ICTs themselves. In line with that position, the main body of this chapter looks at various common components of social work practice (assessment, recording, reviewing and so on) and considers how ICT is being used in the practice of social work itself. Of course, this is a rapidly developing scene. So in order to make sense of it, the chapter first takes a brief look at the development of ICTs themselves, and at changes in UK government policy that have influenced the adoption of ICTs within social work. It also considers future trends and possibilities.

The purpose of the chapter is to prepare the ground for the remainder of the book by presenting a survey of social work contexts in which ICTs are being used. The remainder of the book is concerned with the impact that the use of these ICTs is having on social work as a whole. One of the key tasks will be to assess the extent to which the growing use of ICTs has met the policy objectives that lay behind their introduction. Are they achieving what was intended? Are there unforeseen consequences? This will require some critical thinking about the policy objectives themselves, and about how the impact of ICTs can be assessed. But in this chapter, questions about why ICTs have been introduced into social work are answered only from the perspective of their proponents. In other words, this chapter will report the claims made for the introduction and use of ICTs and later chapters will explore evidence relating to their impact in practice.

First there is a short, introductory account of the available technologies. Second, there is a survey of social work practice that catalogues the various uses of ICT. Finally, there is a brief account of how service users are using ICT for peer support and for campaigning.

What is ICT?

Information and Communication Technology is a broad term that is used to cover all the digital methods by which information is created, stored, manipulated and shared. This includes computer hardware and peripherals of all kinds, and the software and networks that they use to store, process and communicate information. It also includes digital broadcasting and mobile telecommunications technology.

This definition covers all the standard software applications that are in use on individual personal computers in homes and offices; word processing, spreadsheets, presentations, desktop publishing, email and so on. But it is the increasing ease with which electronic data can be transferred to or from individual computers through local networks within organisations, or via the internet, that is producing the most rapid change in social work and elsewhere. For example, Web 2.0 technologies allow service users not only to view 'static' information about services over the internet but also to communicate with others, sometimes in real time, about their experiences of social work services. And sophisticated databases allow providers of social work services to collect information about service users and about how resources are being used, and to share that information with others. It is this second level of technology, moving beyond the individual personal computer, that is of primary interest here. What follows is a brief review of some of the key features of the ICTs that are discussed in this chapter. This is not, of course, an exhaustive list. A basic familiarity with word processing, spreadsheets, presentations, web browsers and email is assumed.

Databases

Databases are used routinely to store and retrieve information, for example, in relation to supermarket product sales. When a purchase is made it is likely that some or all of the following data will be recorded:

- Details of the product itself
- The quantity purchased
- The date and time of the transaction
- The method of payment
- The name of the salesperson
- Customer details

The supermarket holds a record of all the products that they sell and the quantity in stock, so that by entering the data relating to this current sale the new stock level can be calculated and fresh product ordered if needed.

But the supermarket also holds a record of all its salespeople, so that this sale can be credited to the correct person and the productivity of individual staff can be monitored. It can also analyse the data relating to the date and time of sale in order to track sales growth, and it can analyse customer details to hone its marketing strategy. All these quite different functions are achieved by using the same large database, which is actually a series of related tables where each holds information about stock, staff or customers. The multiplicity of potential uses is a key characteristic of complex databases.

A distinction is commonly drawn between 'data' and 'information'. Data can be considered to be the raw material that is 'processed' in order to provide more meaningful information. So the supermarket may collect data about individual transactions, but such data must be processed before information about the age profile of customers buying a particular product can be obtained.

It is possible for small databases to be stored on an individual personal computer. But the power of large, organisational databases is greatly increased by the ability to enter data and retrieve information from any networked computer, whether that is in the warehouse, sales floor or administrative office.

Network technologies

Computers may be linked together using cables, where fibre optic cable gives the fastest transmission speeds, or wirelessly using microwave, satellite or Bluetooth. Various types of networks are mentioned in this book, including:

- *Local area networks (LAN)*. These cover small geographical areas such as a home or office. They may be wired or wireless.
- *Virtual private networks (VPN)*. These are often used to allow secure communication over the public internet, for example to allow home workers to connect to an organisation's network.
- *Intranets*. These are usually networks belonging to specific organisations, where the content is under the control of the organisation and access is restricted to authorised users.
- *The internet*. This is the sum total of all governmental, academic, public and private networks. It provides the communications network for the World Wide Web.

Web 2.0 technologies

The term Web 2.0 reflects the shift away from 'static' web pages towards web applications that allow people to collaborate and share information online. Using Web 2.0 technologies information can be uploaded easily to existing sites. Examples include social networking sites, video sharing sites, wikis and blogs. Some of the key features of Web 2.0 technologies are that:

- They allow self expression that is available to a global audience
- They can bring people together and build communities
- They allow anonymity and identity play
- They present a challenge to some corporate business models (e.g., the music and film industries through peer to peer file sharing) (Gauntlett, 2004).

Online peer reviews of goods and services are having an impact not only in the private sector but also in the delivery of public services.

Call centre technology

Call centres are centralised offices that are used to receive high volumes of telephone requests. As people are able to use more varied means of making requests (email, text messaging, online forms or personal visits) so the concept of the contact centre has evolved, particularly in health and personal social services. Key feature of the ICTs in contact centres are:

- automatic telephone call distribution and 'call waiting' display boards;
- systems for finding and displaying the computerised record relating to known callers;
- systems allowing close monitoring of operators by supervisors.

Government Policy

The election of a New Labour government in the UK in 1997 coincided with a period of rapid expansion of internet capacity and usage in the mid to late 1990s. The government was quick to highlight the significance of what was described optimistically as a 'new age of information [that] offers possibilities for the future limited only by the boundaries of our imagination' (Cabinet Office, 1998: 1). Whilst commentators have argued over the extent and nature of the social and economic changes brought about by new uses of ICT, nonetheless the idea that an 'information revolution' is taking place has become commonplace in political rhetoric.

A major strand of the UK government's response was the commitment to make all government services available electronically. The argument was that the use of ICTs would bring improvements in efficiency, quality, and in ease of access to government services (Hudson, 2002). Citizens would be able to access services at a time and in a place of their choosing. Whether renewing a car tax disc or getting medical advice from an

NHS Direct call centre, ICTs would reduce the need for visits to physical buildings with set opening hours. The government made a commitment in 2000 to making all of its services accessible electronically from 2005 (Cabinet Office, 2000). One of the outcomes of this process is the UK government website www.direct.gov.uk, a central portal for government information and online services.

But it is clear that some face-to-face public services cannot be delivered electronically – at least, not in their entirety. Social work services are an obvious example. In fact the government allowed individual government departments to decide which services could be exempt. At the same time its electronic service delivery targets included a variety of access 'channels', such as internet-enabled mobile phones and telephone call centres (Hudson, 2002). The rather anomalous inclusion of telephone call centres as an example of 'electronic service delivery' within these targets has had a significant impact on social work services, as call centres have been incorporated within the 'contact centre' model of initial access to services in order to meet electronic service delivery targets.

The emergence of Web 2.0 technologies has meant that electronic access to web services is not restricted to allowing the public to view online information (for example, in relation to the services that a local council provides). This is sometimes referred to as digital 'brochureware'. Rather, it allows *interaction* with services, such as when submitting an online tax return. Perhaps of more interest is the possibility of developing 'expert systems', particularly in relation to referral screening. For example, in the 2009 swine flu pandemic, members of the public with the relevant symptoms were able to gain access to anti-viral medication by completing an online questionnaire that was designed, in part, to screen out more serious cases for referral to a GP. The level of expertise inherent in this particular system was low, but it seems likely that online systems with similar low-level expertise may become more widespread in screening referrals to services, perhaps including social work services.

One of the concepts underlying the government's commitment to electronic access to services is that of 'citizen-facing government' (Cabinet Office, 2000). Taking its cue from successful businesses that use e-commerce, the government has sought to manage its relationships with its 'customers' in a similar way. A key feature is that citizens should not have to deal with departments and agencies individually but should be able to update their personal information or make a request at a single electronic 'portal'. This information would then be passed automatically in electronic format to all the relevant service providers. Clearly, this requires data sharing between agencies and is an example of another of the government's major policy objectives: the creation of joined-up services.

The joining up of services through ICTs is not restricted to public sector organisations. The government has encouraged public sector organisations to allow their services to be accessed from, and linked to, commercial websites. And public sector ICT projects are heavily dependent on private sector technical expertise with big, multinational communications companies heavily involved in ICT delivery. Indeed, Hudson argues that 'in developing their plans for e-government, New Labour have effectively decreed that the distinction between public and private matters very little. Instead, the new view seems to be that what "works" is what counts' (2002: 522). Garrett (2005) gives the example of a public–private 'partnership' in the Connexions Service for young people, where an electronic Connexions Card that monitors school attendance also gives rewards that can be redeemed in retail outlets. In this way it seems that the e-agenda is linked to the marketisation of the public sector.

So far this review of government policy has been broad in scope. What of specific government policy developments in relation to social work? A number of significant UK government-driven projects that rely on ICTs should be mentioned here. They will be discussed more fully in the following section. First there is the requirement for local authorities to develop electronic databases for service user records across all service user groups. Second, there is a series of social work assessment tools that started life as paper records and have become, or are in the process of becoming, 'electronic'. Third, there is the development of the Integrated Children's System (ICS) for 'children in need', a system that is heavily dependent on an ICT infrastructure. Finally there is the development of 'ContactPoint', a national database that was intended to hold details of all the children in England and Wales. It is unlikely that these specific initiatives will all have a long shelf-life. Indeed, the demise of ContactPoint was signalled immediately after the election of a new government in May 2010. But the example will serve, because the basic form and intentions of these initiatives will recur in their successors.

Social Work Practice

The International Federation of Social Workers gives the following definition of social work:

> The social work profession promotes social change, problem solving in human relationships and the empowerment and liberation of people to enhance well-being. Utilising theories of human behaviour and social systems, social work intervenes at the points where people interact with their environments. Principles of human rights and social justice are fundamental to social work. (International Federation of Social Workers, 2000)

Later in the book we take a more critical approach to considering the aims, purposes and values of social work, as we consider how the incorporation of ICTs into social work may be changing its practice. But for now we are concerned with something more descriptive. The aim of this section is to identify some of the common components of social work practice, in line with the above definition, and to show how ICTs are being utilised.

Relationships with service users

Many years ago I had a car exhaust repaired by my local branch of a national tyre and exhaust fitters. But they hadn't done the job properly and so, a few days later and far from home, I had a car that once again sounded like a tractor. I wanted it fixed without charge before driving home, but I didn't have the receipt relating to the original repair. Could I persuade a branch that didn't know me that I was a genuine customer with a complaint? I was pleasantly surprised when they simply entered my car registration number into the computer, found the relevant details, and did the work without argument.

This was the first time that I saw the power of what has since become commonplace: the idea that individual customer records can be held centrally and accessed from anywhere by means of a unique identity number (in this case the car registration number). Now we expect to be able to contact any organisation, from our electricity supplier to our favourite retail store, give a customer number or an address and talk to someone who knows all about our situation. Many large organisations have call centres or contact centres just for this purpose, linked to electronic databases containing customer records. But before turning to social work we should perhaps note that our expectations are not always fully met, even in the most consumer-orientated and high-tech organisations.

Many local authority providers of statutory social work services in the UK have introduced contact centres, mainly for first contacts with the agency by telephone, email, text message or, sometimes, in person. If a service user is then allocated a particular social worker, it is usual for them to be given a direct telephone number or email for subsequent contacts. As we have seen, UK government policy has been one of the drivers that have led to the establishment of contact centres. Contact centres may or may not employ qualified social workers but, in any case, their role is effectively one of screening. In a case study of such a centre in the north of England, Coleman (2009) reports the use of the motto 'Resolve, Redirect or Refer'. The study shows that contact centre workers would first try to resolve a person's problem there and then but, failing that, they would either redirect, where appropriate, to another service altogether, or they would accept the referral for a social work service from the local authority and pass it on to the appropriate team.

Contact centres are increasingly being allied to online information about the kind of statutory services that local authorities offer. In many cases this takes the form of static web pages that provide the relevant information. But in some cases local authorities are using Web 2.0 technologies to provide, for example, online self-assessment tools. At the time of writing one English county council allowed adults to complete online needs assessments when they were finding it difficult to manage everyday activities such as climbing stairs, getting in and out of bed or some aspects of personal care. Completing the online assessment results in 'an instant response informing if you, or the person you are completing the assessment for, are eligible for services' (Kent County Council, 2009). Ticking the appropriate boxes then leads straight on to a request for those services, or their cash equivalent in direct payments.

None of this would be possible without a database of service user records. In the early days of computing, during the 1980s, such databases were seen purely as administrative tools. They held basic identifying details of service users, the date of referrals and some basic information about the nature of the problem or request, and they were used to keep track of how long a 'case' had been 'open' and to which social worker. This electronic information was maintained by administrators and kept separate from the 'professional' recording about the work itself (notes of interviews or visits, assessment reports and so on). The latter was undertaken by social workers and kept in a hard copy file. Glastonbury (1985) gives an account of developments during this early period. Since then, databases of service user records have become far more sophisticated in several respects.

First there has been an expansion in the quantity of electronic data that is held about individuals. Modern databases have moved far beyond the recording of basic identifying details to incorporate the 'professional' element of the social work task. They are used to record the details of social workers' contacts with service users and, often, they provide the structure for gathering and analysing information for assessments.

Second, a 'joined-up' approach to services means that there is pressure for databases of service user records to become larger and more interconnected. A good example is the national database known as ContactPoint, planned under a previous UK Labour Government and cancelled by the incoming coalition Government. The relevant UK government website described this as:

> a quick way for practitioners to find out who else is working with the same child or young person, making it easier to deliver coordinated support.

ContactPoint is an online directory, available to authorised staff who need it to do their jobs, enabling the delivery of coordinated support for children and young people. It is also vital to help safeguard children; and to ensure that the right agencies are involved at the right times, so children do not slip through the net. (Department for Children, 2009b)

This account implies two main objectives. First, it was intended to promote collaboration and joint working – being used by all the agencies working with children and their families. Second, by being national and including all children, it would ensure that children do not fall through the net. Note that there has been significant argument about the advantages and disadvantages of such a database, and we will consider these fully in Chapter 4. These issues are always likely to be subject to political uncertainty with changes of national governments (e.g., Mathieson, 2009).

According to the website (Department for Children, 2009b) ContactPoint was intended to mirror earlier practice insofar as it would hold basic information about who was working with a child and would not hold detailed assessment, medical or other case information. It would be primarily an administrative tool. But some other databases of service user records have grown to incorporate 'professional' elements, leading to the creation of 'electronic files'. We will examine electronic record keeping in the next section. But it is important to realise that many local authorities are likely to remain in a state of transition for some years, with 'hard copy' files existing uneasily alongside some electronic record keeping and assessment formats.

Record keeping and accountability

Social workers are expected to keep records of the work that they undertake. This is one way of ensuring accountability to individual service users and, sometimes, to wider society by documenting how decisions are made. In order to do so it is necessary to record factual information, but also to record the development of professional thinking and the resulting professional decisions. It is widely accepted that good practice is to separate, as far as is possible, fact from opinion, although this is rarely as straightforward as it may sound.

Some databases are designed so that social workers can directly record information about their contacts with service users. For example, the Integrated Children's System (ICS) (Department for Children, 2009a) has online forms where social workers must record details of their visits to children who are being looked after by the local authority. The minimum frequency of these 'statutory visits' is specified by regulations that have the full force of law. Although the exact details vary between local authorities, the ICS brings together basic factual recording (date and place of visit and who was present) with an opportunity to record the content of what was discussed with the child and the social worker's impressions.

Note that the ICS employs complex databases in a way that is quite typical: it attempts to fulfil multiple aims simultaneously. There is the professional aim of producing timely and sufficiently detailed recording so that, for example, someone else can continue the work if the allocated social worker is ill. But, arguably, the more significant drivers behind the development of the ICS are managerial or supervisory. By making social workers record their visits to looked-after children on a central database it is easy to monitor their work and to send reminders if they are in danger of not meeting the minimum frequency for statutory visits.

Assessment and decision making

In recent years there have been moves by government to introduce standardised assessment formats into several areas of social work: children's services, youth justice and community care services in particular. All of these assessment formats require certain, pre-defined types of information to be collected before judgements are made about, for example, entitlement of an adult to a community care service, or the risk of a young person reoffending. The formats are designed to ensure comprehensive data collection and to aid structured decision making. The following examples are from England, but parallel examples could be afforded from Scotland, Wales or Northern Ireland:

- In children's services: the *Framework for the Assessment of Children in Need and their Families* (FFA) (Department of Health, 2000) and the *Common Assessment Framework* (CAF) (Department for Children, 2009e)
- In youth justice: the ASSET assessment tool (Youth Justice Board, 2006)
- In community care: the *Single Assessment Process* (SAP) (Department of Health, 2002).

Using these assessment frameworks means filling in forms. This is particularly true at the information collection stage, but some of these frameworks also have forms that are intended to encourage analysis (for example, the summary boxes in relation to each 'domain' in the FFA). So it is not surprising to find that electronic versions of structured assessment frameworks are being developed. For example, the FFA is incorporated within the ICS, the CAF is being developed as the National eCAF (Department for Children, 2009d) and, in London, the SAP has become eSAP (NHS London, 2009).

The use of assessment frameworks in social work has been the subject of much debate, regardless of whether or not ICTs are used to support them. It is argued that the presentation of assessment processes as linear, with one stage following another to a final decision, massively oversimplifies the reality of assessment. For example, Wilson et al. argue that 'the assessment process is a convoluted, backwards and forwards activity that produces a dynamic assessment relevant to the specific time, place and relationship in which it was derived' (2008: 272). In addition, it is argued that such frameworks imply a degree of scientific objectivity that simply does not exist (Milner and O'Byrne, 2002). Later in this book we will explore how, from the perspective of all those involved, the use of ICTs to support assessment processes alters this debate about the nature of social work practice in relation to assessment.

Social work interventions

Most social work interventions work through interpersonal relationships in order to promote change. Indeed, Wilson et al. (2008) make a strong case for the centrality of relationship-based approaches in social work. They argue that social work needs practitioners who can form meaningful professional relationships with service users – relationships that facilitate change. Such interpersonal approaches to intervention seem not only to leave little room for the use of ICTs but also, perhaps, to run counter to the bureaucratisation that they seem to represent. Again, this is a theme that we will explore later in the book. But in this introductory section we should note that there are some ways in which ICTs are being used to intervene either to help people or, in some cases, to control their behaviour.

First, there is online counselling. This is mainly offered by independent, qualified counsellors for a fee. Writing about their own experiences as online counsellors, Jones and Stokes (2009) record that their clients gave the following reasons for choosing to work online, rather than face-to-face: convenience, flexibility, invisibility and having a written record of the work. One might expect these to apply equally in the public sector, and there is some evidence that statutory social work agencies are beginning to develop similar services. For example, Kooth (2009) is a public–private partnership in Manchester, UK, offering free online counselling services to young people.

Second, there is 'telecare'. According to the NHS Choices website telecare is:

any service that brings health and social care directly to a user, generally in their homes, supported by information and communication technology. It covers alarms, lifestyle monitoring and telehealth. (NHS Choices, 2009)

The combination of an ageing population, government pressure to increase the efficiency of service delivery, rapid advances in the technology itself, and decreasing telecommunications costs is leading to the widespread introduction of telecare. The Department of Health has provided £100 million (2006–9) for telecare development (Hanson et al., 2009). In its most basic form, telecare can consist of an alarm button that is worn by a vulnerable person and can be used to summon help. It is linked via a base unit to a telephone line or mobile phone connection. More sophisticated sensors can monitor vital signs such as heart rate or blood pressure and allow a real-time response if there is a sudden change for the worse. Similarly, other sensors can be used to detect falls or floods. But sometimes an individual's well-being deteriorates slowly, without the kind of crisis that might trigger one of these alarms. This is where lifestyle monitoring (LSM) is designed to help. LSM sensors monitor people's daily routines in their own home, for example, in which chair they usually sit and for how long, their use of TV, cooker, and so on. 'Intelligent' systems learn people's normal habits and can recognise significant deviations from the norm and alert a caregiver.

As the NHS Choices website acknowledges, the use of telecare raises the fear that technology will replace face to face care, or that it will be too expensive for people to afford (NHS Choices, 2009). These and other issues relating to the impact of telecare on service users and professionals will be explored in the next two chapters.

Third, ICTs are also used by people with disabilities, particularly to aid communication. Murray and Aspinall make the claim that: 'Many of the problems which arise when one is attempting to include people with disabilities adequately in society can be at least partially solved through the use of IT' (2006: 13). They go on to show how people who cannot speak may communicate via a keyboard in a manner that is emotionally and socially neutral. For those using visual symbols there is a variety of translation software, and speech recognition software can help those who cannot use a keyboard. Later in this book we will examine people's experiences of using ICTs in this way.

As well as these 'helping' interventions, social workers sometimes make use of ICTs to control people's behaviour. Electronic 'tagging' may be used to keep track of young people in England and Wales who are subject to an Intensive Supervision and Surveillance Programme, sentenced to community orders, or released from prison early (Youth Justice Board, 2009). The idea is that curfews can be imposed, during which time the young person must remain indoors, or they can be banned from entering certain areas. At its simplest, a tag is connected to the young person's ankle or wrist and a base unit is connected to the telephone line in their home. If they move out of range of the base unit within specified hours, or if the base unit is removed from the telephone, then an alarm is sent to the operator. Currently, more sophisticated systems using GPS tracking are being trialled. Tagging systems are run and monitored by private companies on contracts. The Youth Justice Board (2009) claims that tagging can prevent young people from hanging out with the wrong crowd, can help to improve family relationships and can bring stability and structure to their lives. However, it acknowledges that tagging works best when combined with 'human' tracking; that is when a volunteer makes regular visits to check, for example, that the young person is going to school.

Evaluation and learning

Social work agencies are making increasing use of ICTs to promote learning within their organisations. Many have internal intranets that are accessible only to their own staff. At the most basic level these are used as a library of information for staff (agency policy documents, links to external sites for further information on specialist topics). But Web 2.0 social features are also being used to create, for example, online staff forums where people in different offices can exchange ideas, or wikis to build a communal body of knowledge. We have more to say in Chapter 7 about how ICTs can support learning in social work agencies.

Remote working

As ICT becomes more embedded in social work tasks, the issue of geographical flexibility becomes more pressing. What happens when a social worker is out of the office, visiting a family, and needs to find out, urgently, whether anyone else is working with a particular child? Returning to the office to log in to the workers' own, dedicated terminal is increasingly unnecessary. ContactPoint, for example, was designed to allow access for designated users over the public internet from any internet-enabled device. But such networked systems raise obvious problems with data security.

Social work agencies in the UK are developing a range of approaches to secure remote working. For example, the Children and Family Court Advisory and Support Service (Cafcass) has signed up to the government wide Flex Shared Services Programme (Fujitsu, 2009). This programme allows public sector organisations access to a deal with Fujitsu to supply a complete secure organisational IT infrastructure, both hardware and software. For Cafcass the top priority in signing up to this £25 million deal to replace the previous IT infrastructure was said to be security for remote working. On the other hand, the Youth Justice Board (YJB) has taken a more incremental approach, encouraging local Youth Offending Teams to install links to case management systems and secure email in local courts, and allowing existing users of 3G-enabled Personal Digital Assistants (PDAs) secure access. The YJB's approach, and their guidance to staff on data security, is published as a leaflet (Youth Justice Board, 2008).

There are other issues posed by remote working. As university academic staff we are familiar with the ways in which the boundaries between our work and private lives are eroded. Whilst the offer of an agency laptop to work from home will be welcomed by some practitioners, for whom it saves time and makes for flexible working, for others it will increase the expectation of managers that work continues out of office hours. We return to this theme in Chapter 6 when we discuss the implications for students and academic staff of 'edgeless' social work programmes.

Use of ICT by Service Users

So far we have considered social work practice and the use of ICT from the perspective of government policy and social work agencies. In Chapter 3 we will consider the evidence about service users' experience of these developments, and how they may be changing social work from the perspective of service users. But before doing so, it is important to acknowledge that users of social work services do more than merely react to the increasing use of ICT by government and social work agencies. Services users are also active users of ICTs. Indeed, service users' uptake of ICTs for peer support, and for campaigning, in particular, is having a significant effect on social work. The impact of this will be considered in Chapter 3. In keeping with the more limited aims of this chapter, this section describes the key features of peer support and campaigning websites and gives some examples.

Peer support

In recent years there has been a growth in online peer support groups, across a wide range of health conditions and traumatic life stages. It has been argued that using such websites promotes self-formation, and that interaction with others affects an individual's sense of self (Orgad, 2004). Examples of such websites include problem gambling (GamAid, 2009), bereavement (GROWW, 2009), bipolar disorder (Depression and Bipolar Support Alliance, 2009), and divorce (DivorceSource, 2009). Indeed, some sites offer a one-stop-shop for a wide range of 'health issues' and 'life challenges' (Daily Strength, 2009; MDJunction, 2009).

Significant features of such sites include:

- *Anonymity*. Sites can often be visited without the need to register – so that the visitor's presence is not visible to other users. Registering usually requires a username, not a real name.
- *Codes of conduct*. Users usually sign up to a code of conduct on registration. Typically, these include agreement not to post any copyrighted material or anything which is threatening, invading of others' privacy, sexually oriented, or that violates any laws.
- *Moderation*. Most sites are 'moderated' – that is to say that those running the site hold the right to remove any material that contravenes the code of conduct.
- *Ownership*. Most sites are open about who has created the site and what the aims are.
- *Availability*. Sites can be accessed at any time of the day. Live chat rooms may only be open at specified times but message boards are always available.
- *Internationality*. Many of these sites are based in the United States, although new sites are emerging in many other countries. Most allow access from other countries and they often have an international user base.

Pressure groups

Some peer support websites are run by organisations that have wider, campaigning aims. For them, a presence on the internet is used to give information about their latest campaigns, with online recruitment, ideas for letters and petitions, and links to other organisations. Lax (2004) argues that this use of the internet is not radically different from previous ways of campaigning, except insofar as it is much more efficient, and it may reach non-members. Examples include disability campaigning organisations such as the National Autistic Society (2009), groups such as Families Need Fathers (2009) and the movement promoting anorexia as a lifestyle choice, rather than an eating disorder, for example, House of Thin (2009).

Taking it further

Exercise

Consider any social work agency that you know – ideally one where you have been on placement as a student – and carry out a review of its use of ICTs. Consider as you do so whether the use of ICTs has implications for the following:

- The relationship between social workers and service users
- Aims and forms of record keeping
- Making assessment and planning decisions
- Social work intervention

If you are on a social work programme, ask your programme staff to arrange an opportunity for you to use your local virtual learning environment to exchange with the course group your conclusions about the patterns of ICT usage you have discovered. If you are unsure of the kinds of arrangements we have in mind, you will find more in Chapter 6.

3

Service Users, Carers and ICT

We aimed in Chapter 1 to set out the basis for a good practice model for social workers in relation to technology in general, and information and communication technologies in particular. Part of our argument in that chapter was about the importance of practice-led technology rather than technology-led practice and thinking. A common way of tackling the field is by reasoning 'Technology claims to offer A, B and C. How can we apply A, B and C to social work?' We describe this as a technology-led approach. This approach is not without merit in certain cases, in that it may push towards new ways of imagining technological challenges to existing practice. But it may also mean that social work practice and thinking becomes dominated by those areas where technology has something to offer, to the neglect of equally or even more important needs and questions.

Taking a practice-led approach it follows that good social work practice in relation to ICT can travel almost no distance at all without hearing the voice of the service user. A practice-led ICT must include central dimensions that are service-user-led. We explore these issues in this chapter, intentionally sequencing it before we consider practitioner or agency issues in the next two chapters.

The chapter falls into four main parts. We start with a discussion of what we know regarding the actual or probable impact of technology and ICT on service users. We range fairly widely over service domains, including disability, older people, mental health and children and families. This discussion poses an important question. Do service users share common ground with practitioners and agencies on the issues discussed in this first part of the chapter? We will set out in the second part of the chapter the grounds for believing that there is reasonable evidence that service user/practitioner priorities are unlikely to be entirely congruent. Following closely from this discussion, we present what we see as the main political and ethical issues in the third part of the chapter. These include ethical concerns regarding consent, confidentiality and privacy, and also questions of whether ICT has a bearing on social work's role in combating social exclusion. We discuss this in the context of the much-debated idea of a digital divide. This connects with Chapter 5 (e.g., whether social work services discriminate through the development and delivery of ICT applications), but there may also be a question of digital divides *within* citizen, carer and service user communities. We devote the final main part of the chapter to a more specific account of user, carer and citizen-led ICT. We have in mind circumstances where ICT resources are at the forefront of and help to define and mediate the nature of the activity, rather than the widely prevalent instances where ICT is used in an almost routine manner, through organisation websites, distribution lists and so on. These include, for example, campaigning and lobbying groups, collective identity networks, and resources set up to be used by and meet user and carer needs and interests.

ICT Impacts on Service Users and Carers

We use the term 'impact' with some hesitation. First, it presumes something that is always 'heavy' and comes with force – a blow, collision, bang or crash. Second, impacts happen in a moment. Third, it seems to imply an inertia or at least passivity on the part of the impacted-upon – a bearing of the brunt. None of these may be true in a generalised way in the field of social work. We will see in our discussion of the example of technology-dependent children below that there is a range of weights in the consequences for children and parents. As for momentary impacts, a distinction is necessary. The word impact is used in two different ways – first to refer to the action itself (the blow or collision), and second to refer to the consequences (the influence, impression or effect). The former is probably momentary, while the latter may be both momentary and long-run. This distinction is not always made clear when social workers or researchers talk about the impact of technological or other aspects of services. Here we are usually talking about impact in the second sense. In the next chapter we discuss how the active work of practice always 'mediates' technology, and where it is rarely helpful to think of practice and the practitioner as passively receiving and being moulded by technology. It is likewise true for the service user, carer and citizen. So neither weight nor instantaneousness nor passivity is true in all instances. Yet we stay with 'impact' because we want to focus on the manifold ways that *technology-led* services or practices do have implications for those on the receiving end, however active and responsive they may be. A further distinction is called for, between an impact that is largely indirect, and one that is largely direct.

Indirect impacts

We outlined in the opening chapter the changes in society since the mid 1990s, such that the terms information society and surveillance society became commonplace. The European Commission even has an 'information society portal' (http://ec.europa.eu/information_society/index_en.htm). In mid 2009 Viviane Reding, the EU's Commissioner for Telecoms and Media, delivered a lecture at a flagship event on economic modernisation on the topic: 'Digital Europe – Europe's Fast Track to Economic Recovery'. The spreading fingers of e-government with the advent of New Labour in the UK in 1997 (Hudson, 2002) have shaped social work in almost all domains, including mental health, children and families, health and disability, and older people. Social workers and others have often raised reasonable critical questions about the potential dark side of such developments (Garrett, 2005; Langan, 2009; Parton, 2008a; Parton, 2008b; Peckover et al., 2008). Take for example mental health. Langan focuses on mental health service users who are thought to pose a risk to other people. She detects within the development of electronic databases a danger of increased surveillance, and suggests that risk assessments may yield more 'false positives' (people who are assessed as a risk to the public when in fact they are not) than 'true positives'. In the children's services field, Garrett (e.g., 2005) has persistently warned of the dangers he sees as inherent in the 'electronic turn'. Emerging research in this same area suggests there is empirical support for at least some of these concerns (Pithouse et al., 2009; Shaw et al., 2009b). One study of the Integrated Children's System in the UK included a focused consideration of the experience and views of children with a disability and their parents (see Example 3.1). Twenty-two families were interviewed (four were joint interviews with both parents; 18 were with the mother) and seven children with a disability (for details see Mitchell and Sloper, 2008).

Example 3.1   Children with disability, carers and electronic records

Although families were interviewed after their assessment/review under the Integrated Children's System (ICS), most had no knowledge of the ICS system, or that their children's services department was piloting new information and recording systems. Despite this lack of information, less than half of the parents wanted more information about the ICS.

None could recollect their children being informed. Although it was apparent that most social workers did not explain or mention ICS to the children this was not viewed as problematic. As both a concept and system of information collecting and recording it was regarded by parents as too abstract for children, especially those with communication difficulties. While many parents had not considered issues around electronic exchange of information, some expressed concern about confidentiality issues and some raised issues of accessibility to their records. Others were pragmatic in remarking that security could not be guaranteed for paper files either.

The potential advantages they foresaw from electronic records were that they would enable social workers (and also professionals from other agencies) to transfer and share information more effectively – especially in the hope that sharing might reduce the need for repetition of information. Parents viewed written reports in a practical manner: as a bureaucratic form to be kept but sometimes of very little interest. Paper records were seen as enabling parents to contribute more easily, whereas with electronic records they saw a greater dependency on social workers or administrators for inputting their comments or making amendments. This seemed to suggest that they saw an electronic shift as bringing with it a greater distance between themselves and the recorded deposit of the service they received.

Parents noted no discernible difference between pre- and post-ICS assessments/ reviews, including the view that social workers had not altered their practice. Only a small number could remember signing a copy of their recently conducted ICS assessment, although it emerged that signing is currently not routine practice; neither was it viewed as a matter of concern by parents (Mitchell and Sloper, 2008).

As with developments in the health and children's services sectors, how older people 'engage with and are perceived by the services and systems they encounter is increasingly shaped by information technology' (Hardey and Loader, 2009: 660). Hardey and Loader helpfully connect two important dimensions when explicating the issues in this field: the extent to which service users are engaged, and the degree to which health and social care services have become integrated. They believe that services have become increasingly integrated and that 'information technology systems are increasingly shared by health and social care practitioners who have access to more or less integrated databases' (p. 662). It is quite possible that in England an important lead in this regard will prove to have been given by the central government Department of Health, and we review some of their initiatives in the next chapter. However, Hardey and Loader underline that older people have thus far been more or less excluded from the development and implementation of new systems:

> To put it starkly, older people remain represented as subjects of information, as practitioners largely mediate their information needs. In this sense, older people remain a source of data rather than as partners in the creation and management of both their data and the way it is used by practitioners and organizations. (Hardey and Loader, 2009: 663)

This illustrates how, while one area of agreed good service development may move forward (in this example, integration) it is quite possible that it can be associated with a growth in 'informatisation' that marginalises the older person as a participant in the system.

Direct impacts

Information-led services for older people are not restricted to broad-scale programme initiatives, but may also include circumstances where technology is deeply embedded in the direct service delivery. One example is the area of assistive technology (AT), i.e., products or services that are designed to enable older people or people with a disability to remain in the community. Various benefits have been claimed for such services. These are said to include (Beech and Roberts, 2008: 3):

- increased choice, safety, independence and sense of control;
- improved quality of life;
- maintenance of ability to remain at home;
- reduced burden placed on carers;
- improved support for people with long-term health conditions;
- reduced accidents and falls in the home.

There is some evidence in support of these benefits. 'Users of AT have identified the benefits and downsides to their experiences of AT. Many of the benefits relate to wellbeing and confidence in living independently rather than to direct health benefits, but have been shown to be important in the package of care delivered' (Beech and Roberts, 2008: 7).

Some helpful work has been done in a corresponding area, in understanding families' experiences of caring for 'technology-dependent' children (Heaton et al., 2005). We realise that this example is not narrowly about *information* or *communication* technology, but we introduce it because it has a lot to say about the relationship between technology, the lives of carers and service users, and practitioners. Unlike too much work in this field it helps to enrich understanding by theorising the way the social organisation of time is central to service users. For the 36 families in the study, various methods were used to obtain the perspectives of the children, their siblings and their parents, and in all 75 children and adults were interviewed. The authors distinguish between different ways in which time was 'framed', including the natural biological body rhythms, clock time, institutional time (the schedules of service providers, etc.), and what they call 'technological time'. This includes, for example, how long it takes devices to perform their functions (e.g., a kidney dialysis machine) and the associated 'technical care' routines that needed to be performed, usually by carers.

'Technical care' involved a range of activities in a variety of settings. One part of life that was tied to this was sleep. Parents were often faced with the need to administer treatment and/or manage the technology during the nights. A major cause of sleep disturbance was dialysis machines and feeding pumps alarming when the tubes kinked or were blocked when the children lay on them (Heaton et al., 2006).

They 'consider how the incompatibility of these time frames contributes to the social exclusion of families with technology-dependent children from aspects of social life' (Heaton et al., 2005: 442). For example, while some children used devices on a regular and predictable pattern,

> many children also used devices on a more irregular and unpredictable basis which could not be scheduled, and hence families found it difficult to commit themselves to regular activities such as paid work and to plan ahead for holidays. (Heaton et al., 2005: 445)

In their opening up of the meanings of different time frames, Heaton and colleagues pose a range of challenges for social work practitioners and students. Their interesting work recalls an invaluable book from the previous generation about families who cared for children with severe learning disabilities at home (Bayley, 1973). Bayley set out, in a research-grounded way, how families develop a 'structure of coping' where the management of time is crucial. We pick up the question of the ways technology-embedded services can be associated with social exclusion later in this chapter.

User and Professional Views and Priorities

In the light of what is beginning to emerge regarding the impact of ICT, we need to consider two questions. First, what do we know regarding whether the attitudes of service users and carers are similar to those of professionals delivering services, and second, how should we both understand and respond to the special ethical issues that arise for those involved in this field? We will consider the first of these questions in this section, and address the second one in part of the next section. An important issue raises its head at this point, with regard to potential conflicts between service users' and practitioners' respective views of the place and nature of ICT and related assistive technology. Some of the earliest work came with the London government's experiments with electronic tagging of offenders from the 1980s. Electronic monitoring has become an integral part of the criminal justice process in England and Wales. Since the first trials in the 1980s the range of applications of electronic monitoring and the number of offenders subject to it have increased. Early responses from professionals in the probation field were largely critical (e.g., Nellis, 1991). Concerns have continued to be expressed, both about the role of the media and popular culture (e.g., Nellis, 2003) and about the perceived role of the state as extending forms of 'digital rule' (Jones, 2000). Later work focused on the implications of the advent of global tracking technology (e.g., Nellis, 2005). The gradual mainstreaming of electronic tagging has been associated with a gradual shift to accepting it as part of the criminal justice world. In a more recent study Hucklesby suggests that

> for some offenders curfew orders reduce offending and contribute to desistance by addressing levels of social capital in two ways. First, by decreasing levels of anti-social capital by reducing offenders' links with situations, people, places and networks correlated with their offending. Second, by improving levels of pro-social capital by encouraging offenders to connect or re-connect with influences linked with desistance such as family and employment. Curfew orders can also have negative impacts on pro-social capital particularly by disrupting employment and family ties and responsibilities. (Hucklesby, 2008: 51)

She concludes that curfew orders have the potential to play a positive and distinctive role in supporting desistance.

However, with the partial exception of Hucklesby's work, none of this material considers whether the views of professionals and those on the receiving end are similar. Most of the work addressing this question has stemmed so far from the wider social care and health fields. For example, Beech and Roberts, in their briefing on assistive technology and older people (2008), concluded that privacy, freedom from interruption, and reluctance to accept change to the fabric of one's home are all factors that may make older people unwilling to agree to assistive technology, hence posing familiar ethical dilemmas for social workers. We present two helpful examples. First, from a study of professional and patient attitudes to using mobile phone technology to monitor asthma (Pinnock et al., 2006) and second from a research paper that sheds valuable light on the attitudes of family and professional caregivers towards the use of GPS for tracking people with dementia (Landau et al., 2009).

Monitoring asthma

Immediate action in response to severe asthma attacks is important and may even prove life-saving. This sometimes takes place based on written action plans, through which patients take on responsibility for monitoring and adjusting their treatment. A problem may arise if patients do not respond to cues for self-management, or if they delay important actions pending the advice of a clinician. New technologies may prove helpful. Pinnock and her colleague describe 'an asthma monitoring service which enables electronic peak flow readings to be transmitted to a central server which feeds back information on current control and reminders on self-management' (Pinnock et al., 2006: 238). However, utilisation of such developments depends on both patient and professional attitudes to the potential benefits of such initiatives, as well as their 'user-friendliness'.

Both patients and professionals were positive in their attitude to new technology in general, though patients had more diverse views than professionals.[1] Patients were keener than professionals to try the mobile phone technology, and in general thought the technology would help their doctor or asthma nurse look after their asthma, whereas professionals were more sceptical and 'generally neutral about the impact on care' (p. 243). However, both patients and professionals were divided on how the technology would impact on the patient/professional relationship. Would it increase communication or reduce face-to-face contact? Would it increase dependence or facilitate autonomous self-management? There were also concerns on both sides about who would bear the cost and what the time implications would be.

Tracking people with dementia

It will be clear from the asthma example that either/or conclusions about user and professional attitudes regarding the benefits of ICT are likely to oversimplify. This conclusion is underlined by the results of an important study in Israel of the use of more advanced electronic tracking such as GPS (Global Positioning Systems) for elderly people with dementia (Landau et al., 2009).[2] The lives of older people with dementia can be threatened should

---

[1]Questionnaire replies were received from 130 of 300 professionals (43%) and 202 of 389 patients (52%).
[2]The results were drawn from data collected from 69 family caregivers and 96 professional caregivers.

they wander. Wandering is also an added source of distress for family caregivers, and a cause of exhaustion for professional staff members caring for people in nursing units. Would electronic tagging technologies offer an increased range of options for maintaining the safety and welfare of vulnerable individuals, or would they threaten personal autonomy and liberty?

The authors distinguish five different fields where attitudes were manifested:

- use for the sake of person's safety;
- use for caregivers' peace of mind;
- respecting elders' autonomy;
- supporting restricted use in certain circumstances;
- opposition to all use.

Professionals and caregivers held significantly different views on all five of these attitudes. Within this, the differences were complex and do not lend themselves to easy generalisation. The authors summarise the 'remarkable' differences between the two groups as follows:

> Family caregivers showed significantly higher support for the use of GSP and RFID [Radio Frequency Identification] than professional caregivers, both for their own peace of mind and for the safety of the elderly they cared for … On the other hand, professionals attached significantly higher value to respect for a person's autonomy and restricted support for using GS and RFID. This is to say that family caregivers value their own peace of mind and their relatives' safety more than the autonomy of the latter. (Landau et al., 2009: 685)

Yet family caregivers were significantly more opposed to the use of this device than professional caregivers. There was a variety of evidence consistent with a view that the use of tracking devices may be contrary to human dignity, particularly due to its invasion of privacy. The authors conclude that we need to think differently about caregivers' views:

> Instead of the dichotomous attitude of either favouring or opposing the use of such a device, the results … suggest a more complex approach, according to which caregivers' attitudes range from obligation to use the tracking device for the sake of patients' safety through support of the use of the device for the sake of the caregivers' peace of mind and restricted support, to objection to the use of the device and respect for a person's autonomy. (pp. 683–4)

Perhaps not surprisingly, all the evidence we have thus far cautions against assuming that service users and carers will take a similar view of ICT and social work to those held by practitioners. But more importantly, it also suggests that generalisations about the specifics of user and carer attitudes and interests are unlikely to be plausible.

One caution should be entered. In the case of any given ICT innovation we need to consider whether responses are likely to persist or shift. There is general agreement that technology implementation follows an identifiable life cycle. Early stages may divide between innovators and early adopters, with a more sceptical majority. As a consequence it is often difficult to distinguish those problems which are 'teething problems' and that are likely to be resolved, from those problems that are of the nature of the system. This issue was a major source of dispute between a research team evaluating the Integrated Children's System and the government funders that led eventually to the funders declining to accept the research team's report (Bell et al., 2007). It is likely to be even more difficult for service users with limited access to draw conclusions about this question.

Ethics, Users, ICT and Social Exclusion

Service users and carers hold a range of views about the impacts of ICT that do not always coincide with those of professionals. This means that we need to find ways of making sense of the competing views. For example, we have seen how family members caring for people with dementia are more strongly in favour of the use of GPS tracking systems than are the professionals. This was said to be because family members 'value their own peace of mind and their relatives' safety more than the autonomy of the latter' (Landau et al., 2009: 685). How should we respond to this, and to similar differences of view?

This question takes us into the realm of ethics. Our argument is that ethical questions about the impacts of ICT in social work should be considered in the same way as any other ethical question in social work. This is in line with a practice-led, rather than a technology-led, approach. Influential statements of social work ethics are provided by the International Federation of Social Workers (IFSW, 2005), the British Association of Social Workers (BASW, 2002) and, in the US, by the National Association of Social Workers (NASW, 2008). Of particular relevance to the current discussion are the issues of consent, confidentiality and privacy. We will consider them in turn.

Informed consent

The general ethical principles relating to informed consent are clear. These can be stated briefly as follows (NASW, 2008):

- Valid, informed consent to a social work intervention is required unless: a) the service user lacks the capacity to give it or, b) the intervention has a legal mandate that overrides the service user's wishes.
- Informed consent is based on a clear understanding of the purpose of the intervention, any associated risks, the requirements of any third parties, relevant costs, reasonable alternatives, the time frame, and the right to withdraw consent.
- When a service user lacks the capacity to provide informed consent, then consent should be sought from appropriate third parties. Social workers should ensure that any third party is acting in a manner consistent with the service user's wishes and interests.
- When an intervention is imposed, then the service user should still know about the aims and extent of the intervention, and should understand the consequences of non-compliance.

The introduction of ICT into social work practice does not change these principles, but it leads to new contexts in which they must be applied. Consider the example of an older person consenting to the use of assistive technologies in their own home. We have already seen the reported benefits of assistive technology in increasing people's confidence in their ability to live independently (Beech and Roberts, 2008). But we noted that some older people may be unwilling to accept such technologies because of concerns about physical alterations to the fabric of their homes. Running cables, for example, can cause much disruption. In this situation it is clear that social workers should not conceal or minimise the need for such alterations in their desire to gain the benefits of assistive technology. Informed consent means that older people should understand the full extent of the proposed intervention before agreeing to it, or not.

Tagging of young offenders (Hucklesby, 2008) is an example of a situation in which an intervention is imposed because of a legal mandate. Here, the context relates to a new technology, but the ethical requirement to give information about the extent of the intervention and the consequences of non-compliance is unchanged.

The tracking of people with dementia (Landau et al., 2009) is an example of a situation in which consent may be sought from relatives or carers if the person with dementia lacks the capacity for informed consent. Here the social worker must ensure that such people are acting in line with the wishes and interests of the person with dementia, and not simply so as to gain the personal 'peace of mind' that is likely to be associated with more intrusive intervention. We acknowledge that it may be difficult to distinguish carers' interests in gaining 'peace of mind' from the interests of the person with dementia, and that this is skilled work. But the point is that the ethical basis for decision making has not changed with the introduction of an intervention that utilises ICT.

Confidentiality and privacy

Once again, we must first consider the general ethical principles in relation to confidentiality and privacy before we can apply them to the use of ICT. Key principles are (NASW, 2008):

- Social workers should respect service users' right to privacy.
- Social workers should protect the confidentiality of all information obtained in the course of their work, except for compelling professional reasons or on the basis of a legal requirement. The general exception is the need to prevent serious, foreseeable, and imminent harm to a service user or other identifiable person. In all instances, social workers should disclose the least amount of confidential information necessary to achieve the desired purpose.
- Social workers should inform service users, to the extent possible, about the disclosure of confidential information and the potential consequences, when feasible before the disclosure is made.
- Social workers should discuss with service users and other interested parties the nature of confidentiality and limitations of service users' right to confidentiality as soon as possible in the working relationship.

In relation to consent, we argued that the use of ICT creates new contexts in which established ethical principles must be applied. The same is true in relation to confidentiality and privacy, except that here the communicative power of ICT means that the risks associated with breaches of data security are much higher. Losing a paper file may result in information about one individual becoming known to a few others. Breach of data security in a large, online, database of service user records could result in thousands of records appearing on the internet. In this respect, the parents reported in Mitchell and Sloper's (2008) study may have been unduly sanguine in concluding that concerns about electronic data security are balanced by the recognition that paper files can also be mislaid.

The increasing use of ICTs in social work has not changed the ethical basis of practice in relation to confidentiality and privacy, but it has raised the stakes. Social work service providers are beginning to prioritise electronic data security in a way that was previously unheard of. For example, as we saw in Chapter 2, the Children and Family Court Advisory and Support Service (Cafcass) has introduced a secure organisational IT infrastructure, both hardware and software, where the main priority is data security, including security for remote working via the internet (Fujitsu, 2009).

Social exclusion and the digital divide

Social work has a commitment to the principle of social justice. The International Federation of Social Workers, in its statement on ethics in social work, puts it like this:

Social workers have a responsibility to promote social justice, in relation to society generally, and in relation to the people with whom they work. This means: ...

3 *Distributing resources equitably.* Social workers should ensure that resources at their disposal are distributed fairly, according to need.
4 *Challenging unjust policies and practices.* Social workers have a duty to bring to the attention of their employers, policy makers, politicians and the general public situations where resources are inadequate or where distribution of resources, policies and practices are oppressive, unfair or harmful. (IFSW, 2005)

We need to consider the nature of any relationship between the above responsibilities and the increasing use of ICT in social work. A crucial concept is that of the 'digital divide'. This term has been in use since the mid 1990s to describe a range of policy debates about access to the internet in particular. Many commentators have noted a lack of clarity in the use of this term (Couldry, 2000) or, at the very least, they have pointed to the way in which it has been used at the local and global levels. So, as Norris (2001) argues, there is a 'global divide' between countries in their very different levels of telecommunications infrastructure, numbers of websites hosted, and the numbers of computers and telephones per head of population. This is matched by what Norris calls a 'social divide' within countries, where some people have access to the internet and digital resources and others do not. Research into the social divide, mainly in the USA, has shown that there are significant differences in the amount of time spent online that broadly match other, well established inequalities: for example between rich and poor; town and country; non-disabled people and disabled people; gender, white people and ethnic minorities; younger people and older people. Some have claimed that the social divide in volume of internet usage will disappear as the price of technology falls (Castells, 2001). Yet recent studies have shown that simple measures of the amount of time spent online do not adequately reflect the significance of what people choose to do when they are online. For example, a recent study of civic engagement in local politics in the USA has shown how:

Contrary to the hopes of some advocates, the internet is not changing the socio-economic character of civic engagement in America. Just as in offline civic life, the well-to-do and well-educated are more likely than those less well off to participate in online political activities such as emailing a government official, signing an online petition or making a political contribution. (Smith et al., 2009)

And, closer to home, a study of the ways in which UK internet users gain access to healthcare information (Wyatt et al., 2005) shows how it is not enough to consider just people's physical access to the internet and their IT skills. For example, several of the women in the study reported that their male partners or sons used the home computer to such an extent that the women resorted to seeking health information on a library computer, or at work. Yet research using data about the number of households with internet access would categorise such women as having access at home.

It would seem that, as social work agencies make information about their services available online, and even some of the services themselves, there is an increasing risk that service users may be on the wrong side of the digital divide and unable to gain access to them. However, patterns of internet usage are complex and changing and there is no simple correlation between other forms of social exclusion and the notion of a digital divide. As we will see in the next section, groups of people who are often considered to be socially excluded, such as disabled people, have made extensive use of the internet for campaigning purposes. This raises the possibility that there might be divides *within* these groups, perhaps along the lines of class, making it difficult to predict who might be excluded and in what circumstances. At this stage in the development of online social work services it seems that, at the very least, social work's commitment to social justice means that it is incumbent on agencies to work to understand patterns of ICT usage by service users.

User, Carer and Citizen-led ICT

At the end of Chapter 2 we gave some examples of peer-support websites, and of organisations that make use of the internet in their campaigning and lobbying. In this section we start from the example of Shaping Our Lives: the National User Network for England in which professionals also play a role, before moving on to consider the use of ICT solely by service users, and finally the online dangers to some, particularly children.

Shaping Our Lives

Shaping Our Lives (http://www.shapingourlives.org.uk/index.html) is notable for the way in which it is using Web 2.0 technology such as Facebook and other social networking sites to create a national network of diverse, user-led organisations that aim to improve the quality of support that people receive, by promoting local user involvement. The use of ICT reflects the aims and purposes of the organisation, so we need to consider both together.

Shaping Our Lives is an independent, user-controlled organisation, think tank and network that has been in existence since 2002. Its website lists the following aims:

- support the development of local user involvement that aims to deliver better outcomes for service users
- give a shared voice to user-controlled organisations
- facilitate service user involvement at a national level
- work across all user groups in an equal and accessible manner
- improve the quality of support people receive
- enable groups to link to other user-controlled groups
- develop links with world-wide international user-controlled organisations

and values:

- reflect the priorities and needs of its member organisations
- encourage user-controlled organisations to learn both from each other and from wider best practice
- reflect the diversity of the network in its work
- apply equal opportunities practice in its governance, practice and as an employer. (Shaping Our Lives, 2010)

The aim of making links between user-controlled organisations, so that they can learn from one another, and develop a shared voice, has led to the creation of a dedicated networking site, known as SOLNET, at http://www.solnetwork.org.uk/. User-controlled organisations are able to register as 'members' of the network and non-user-controlled organisations can register as 'friends'. Anyone is able to search the network database for contact details and links to the websites of organisations registered in either category. In addition, members and friends are able to post items to the website's noticeboard. Over the past two years, a wide variety of information has been posted advertising events, campaigns, job vacancies and the latest newsletters.

This site has been developed in collaboration with the Social Care Institute for Excellence (SCIE). This collaboration is interesting insofar as this is not a user-controlled organisation. SCIE 'is an independent charity, funded by the Department of Health and the devolved administrations in Wales and Northern Ireland. SCIE identifies and disseminates the knowledge base for good practice in all aspects of social care throughout the United Kingdom' (Social Care Institute for Excellence, 2010). SCIE claims to 'recognise the central role of people who use services' and has provided funding and technical support for the development of the SOLNET site.

Of interest to both organisations has been the role of service users in the training of professional social workers. This has been a mandatory element of social work education since 2002. Shaping Our Lives has seen user involvement as a major opportunity to improve the support offered to service users. SCIE has prepared a series of relevant reports (Branfield, 2009; Social Care Institute for Excellence, 2009; Taylor et al., 2009). The shared interest has led to the creation of the Social Work Education Participation (SWEP) website at http://www.socialworkeducation.org. uk/. Once again, this is a site where registered service user organisations can post information – this time about their activities in relation to social work education. But this site is also open to Higher Education Institutions and is an example of an online collaboration, backed by SCIE. We will return to the use of ICT in social work education in Chapters 6 and 7.

ICT use by citizens and service users

The examples we have sketched so far in this part of the chapter have been of cases where there is an active role for social workers. There are, of course, other instances where the motivation and drive for online networks and conversations are initiated and maintained *solely* by citizens and service users. The 1998 book by the *Sunday Times* journalist, Ruth Picardie, *Before I Say Goodbye*, charted with searing honesty her life from her diagnosis of cancer until her death. Ruth was the daughter of social workers, although the reason we mention it in the context of ICT is that the book consists almost entirely of her email correspondence, which affords the book an immediacy that pre-electronic forms of writing would have found difficult to sustain. Hardey's depiction of personal accounts of illness on the internet is a further telling example of how this genre has developed (Hardey, 2002).

Other examples of citizen websites fall more into the categories of mutual support or campaigning, in some cases drawing on the developments in Web 2.0 that we outlined in the previous chapter and discuss in detail in Chapter 6. Hardey and Loader's presentation of developments in the informatisation of older people illustrates this (e.g., Hardey and Loader, 2009: 664ff.). A starker example can be seen in pro-anorexia (pro-ana) websites. 'So if you ever want to eat something, remember how you look like and what you can look like', so read the words on the final slide on a MySpace video sequence of still photographs of teenage girls on a pro-anorexia website. It had followed an earlier slide warning viewers

'Remember, Nobody wants a fat girlfriend', and all shown to the accompaniment of a song extolling 'beauty from my pain'. The philosophy of such sites is that anorexia is a lifestyle that young women have intentionally undertaken. By sharing influential rhetoric, 'trigger' images, and dieting tips, site members thereby reconceptualise their experience of anorexia (Richardson and Cherry, 2005).

The source of research information about networks such as those in the pro-ana community illustrates the special difficulties surrounding the ethics of consent, confidentiality, privacy and access when doing internet research (cf. Brotsky and Giles' (2007) covert study of pro-anorexia members). There are three key questions. Can we treat all information taken from the internet as public information? We think probably not, though this is far from agreed. Waruszynski (2002) and Kitchen (2002) give contrary answers. Second, are we free to exploit fully the results to which we have unfettered access? How does informed consent relate for example to material taken from chat rooms, or from listservs? Are there special issues of group consent? How can these be dealt with, assuming it is a real problem? Third, when it comes to interpretation and dissemination, who owns the story? We are not convinced that the same standards ought to apply to, for example, the material on a moderated discussion list or newsgroups and, say, a breast cancer survivors list.

Protecting children in the virtual world

As children and young people make increasing use of the internet there are clearly many positive opportunities to communicate with others in distant places, make new friends, be creative and learn new skills. But there are also risks as children encounter illegal content, or are exposed to harassment or bullying, find their personal data misused or find that they are groomed for sexual purposes.

The UK charity Beatbullying (http://www.beatbullying.org/index.html) has researched children's experiences of online bullying and their report reaches the following conclusions:

- Websites that are popular with children should have a single, industry standard point of contact for reporting misconduct and more transparency about the action taken by service providers in response to such reports
- But, recognising that regulation cannot entirely solve the problem, it recommends the creation of targeted intervention programmes – a 'safety net' – for those most seriously affected. These should include counsellor services, advice sites and online peer support
- There should be increased education for young people about bullying and proper 'netiquette'. (Beatbullying, 2009)

The United Nations organisation, the International Communications Union, not only coordinates international communications infrastructure but also plays a role in relation to child protection. It has issued guidelines for children, parents and educators, industry and for policymakers on online child protection (ITU, 2009). The guidelines for children include 'Smart' rules – where the initials cover advice on:

- Setting your limits – this gives advice about privacy settings and harassment
- Meeting friends offline
- Accepting invitations or friendships
- Reacting to distressing content or bad behaviour
- Telling people about any concerns. (ITU, 2009)

When it comes to protecting children's personal data, a useful summary of the law on children's consent to data sharing, and recommendations for change, has been published by the organisations Action on Rights for Children and the Nuffield Foundation (Dowty and Korff, 2009).

On the question of online sexual exploitation, social workers will gain by being aware of the valuable online resource provided through the Child Exploitation and Online Protection Centre (http://www.ceop.gov.uk/). Research by Quayle and colleagues (2008) for the third World Congress against Sexual Exploitation of Children and Adolescents explores what is known about adult sexual offending online and those who engage in it. It acknowledges that little is known about the children who are victimised and whose images are posted. It suggests that the efficacy of giving safety advice to children (such as by the ITU above) should be systematically evaluated. It further recommends that systems should be put in place internationally for effective investigation, assessment, intervention, support and follow-up when abuse is indicated.

Taking it further

Group exercise

This exercise is for practitioners and students. But if your agency or course is able to invite two or three people who care for technology-dependent children, that would greatly enhance the value of the exercise.

   Obtain copies of the following article and read it:

(Continued)

(Continued)

Heaton, J., Sloper, P. and Shah, R. (2005) 'Families' experience of caring for technology-dependent children: A temporal perspective', *Health and Social Care in the Community*, 13(5): 441–450.

If it is not feasible to either obtain or expect everyone to read this article there is a short summary that can be downloaded from: http://www.york.ac.uk/inst/spru/pubs/rworks/aug2003.pdf

Discuss the practice implications of the main results, and explore how far agreement can be reached between service users, carers and practitioners regarding the benefits and costs of technology dependency.

4

Technology and Professional Practice

Social workers, so it has been expressed by UK higher education authorities, should have knowledge and understanding about 'the implications of modern communication and information technology for service delivery' and 'should be able to use C & IT methods and techniques for a variety of purposes including professional communications, data storage and retrieval and information searching' (Quality Assurance Agency, 2000: 3.1.2 and 3.2.1). The Benchmark reference to 'professional communication, data storage and retrieval, and information searching' indeed includes important implications of ICT for social work practice, but it is far from comprehensive or adequate. In this chapter we aim to set out a vision for ICT and social work practice that follows from the pathway we have trodden so far, and is extensive and analytical, laying the groundwork for an understanding of social work that recognises that technology is endemic, for good or ill, in all social work. It should be read in connection with the following chapter where agency-wide patterns of service delivery are under the spotlight, and the previous chapter, in which we endeavoured to hear the voice of service users, carers and citizens.

At the time of writing, the document setting out the roles and tasks of social workers in the UK is under revision, and the codes of practice and terms for registration for social care workers do not refer to information and communication technology.[1] By contrast, the code of ethics for social workers in the USA is relatively full in recognising the implications of

---

[1] Potentially far reaching developments in the wake of the Baby Peter case have yet to be resolved, although sustained criticism of government ICT systems in children's services during 2009 is likely to lead to an increased concern with how ICT systems in social work influence practice. Chapter 5 has more to say on this theme.

technology within practice. As part of the statement about informed consent, the code says:

> 1.03 (e) Social workers who provide services via electronic media (such as computer, telephone, radio, and television) should inform recipients of the limitations and risks associated with such services.

> 1.03 (f) Social workers should obtain clients' informed consent before audiotaping or videotaping clients or permitting observation of services to clients by a third party.

As part of the statement on privacy and confidentiality the code stipulates that

> 1.07 (m) Social workers should take precautions to ensure and maintain the confidentiality of information transmitted to other parties through the use of computers, electronic mail, facsimile machines, telephones and telephone answering machines, and other electronic or computer technology. Disclosure of identifying information should be avoided whenever possible.

> 1.07 (n) Social workers should transfer or dispose of clients' records in a manner that protects clients' confidentiality and is consistent with state statutes governing records and social work licensure. (NASW, 2008)

This chapter, like Gaul, is divided into three parts.[2] We conclude this introduction by clearing the ground, and by exploring how the social work role, as with some other professions, has come to be seen as defined in significant part by the creation and management of information. The longest part of the chapter outlines and illustrates various ways in which ICT manifests itself in social work practice, whether as an *adjunct* to practice or as a dimension of *direct service delivery*. Finally, we set out what we see as the main practice issues, challenges, opportunities and potential troubles. We suggest ways of continuing critical reflection and practice development.

Ways In

Social workers have varying levels of comfort with technology. Securing employer support to undertake the European Computer Driving Licence is one option. The website for the international computing certification programme can be found at: http://www.ecdl.com/publisher/index.jsp

---

[2]The reference is to Caesar's opening to his Commentaries on the Gallic Wars that 'Gaul is divided into three parts'

If this is not feasible, valuable aspects of ICT skills can be acquired by completing the well-established Internet Social Worker Tutorial: http://www.vts.intute.ac.uk/tutorial/socialwork developed by the Social Care Institute for Excellence (http://www.scie.org.uk/). A tutorial also exists on the same site for health and social care.

The Open University has a free-to-use module on learning social work practice that provides an easy-going exercise of newly acquired skills. This – or any of a number of alternatives – can be traced from: http://openlearn.open.ac.uk/course/category.php?id=11 (all sites accessed 13 May 2010).

Ground Clearing

ICT and social work practice is no longer a greenfield site and, before we get into the specifics, some clearing of the undergrowth is called for. We can summarise this ground clearing in rather paradoxical ways as follows. Social work is in some senses a technology-free zone. Unlike, for example, surgeons (or tree surgeons), nurses, anaesthetists, plumbers, general practitioners or even increasingly teachers, it is only a slight exaggeration to say that social work 'practices depend on using social behaviours (including all aspects of thinking and speaking) as their only tools' (Felleman, 2005). However – paradox one – technology always mediates practice. There are familiar and ubiquitous forms of such practice-mediation that are often almost invisible because they are so taken for granted, from pencil and paper to cell phone, email, two-way clinical observation mirrors, or the mutual recording required of some forms of intervention such as task-centred work. But there are also newer forms that may be experienced as strange and possibly challenging to widely accepted ideas of professional identity and values, and which link back to some of the themes in the previous chapter of this book.

Some observers detect changes in the forms of knowledge in social work from the 'social' to the 'informational', expressed as a shift from a narrative to a database way of thinking (e.g., Parton, 2008b). The thrust of policy innovation is to *separate* knowledge from the knowledge worker and make it something that can be manipulated independently. In this way the user of information technology is disciplined by it.

(T)he 'information-age' is believed to have shifted our lives more towards the world of networks (virtual and actual) in which knowledge is defined by its utility and by its partializing, standardizing and universalizing functionality. (Pithouse et al., 2009: 603–4)

This is most commonly achieved through IT systems that seek to capture and codify knowledge. Insofar as this is true, there is a constant tension between knowledge as residing in people's heads and knowledge as 'downloadable', transferable and open to comparison with other cases. This is a helpful way of thinking about developments in social work, where there is without doubt a growing emphasis on standardisation and formalisation of service delivery. But it should not be overstated. Hence – paradox two – practice always mediates technology, such that technology rarely if ever *replaces* existing practice. Nor is it easily imposed on practitioners. For example, rational, standardised technical forms are unlikely to replace or seriously subvert the exercise of professional discretion, judgement and reflection. Evans and Harris have well reminded us of the irony that the 'existence of rules is not inevitably the death-knell of discretion. Rather, by creating rules organisations create discretion' (Evans and Harris, 2004: 993). We are not sure how many appeals to Donald Schön by advocates of reflective practice are founded on a careful reading of his best-known book (Schön, 1983). Schön's illuminating comparison of superficially contrasting professions – none of which actually included social work – plausibly shows how professionals working in very different fields appear to exercise discretion and reflective practice, even those, like architects and librarians, for whom technology is part and parcel of routine practice.

Taken together – technology mediates practice and practice mediates technology – we should see technology as itself a practice. It is something that practitioners accomplish, rather than being a 'thing'. This is not the usual way practitioners see technology. For example, in a group of practitioners discussing their involvement in a practitioner research network, one member referred to an audio transcription machine.

Lesley[3]:   Can I just add one thing – I am slightly worried about technology. I mean, I still don't know about where we get a thingy ...

Lorna: [Service Director] has one if you want one

Lesley: ... and I am just confused.

We return to these questions during the chapter. But for the moment we illustrate the range of practice contexts for ICT.

Knowing and Understanding Social Work

We noted that the Benchmark statement about social work specified professional communications, data storage and retrieval, and information searching as the illustrations of the practice areas where the exchange with ICT

---

[3]Names are anonymised

would be primarily exhibited. We do not recommend the Benchmark expression as entirely helpful on this point. It is mechanism-led rather than practice-led. One way of summarising the Benchmark approach is that it presents ICT as acting as an adjunct to social work practice, which affords various forms of knowledge and understanding which can in turn be applied to, or within, practice. An additional way of viewing ICT is to express it as part and parcel of direct practice – of assessment, planning, intervention, recording, reviewing or evaluating. We consider each of these in the following paragraphs.

Adjuncts to Good Practice

The various forms such resources take include:

- Gaining access to information and knowledge for practice;
- Developing an understanding of evidence for practice;
- Enhancing or acquiring practice skills;
- Engaging in networking.

Information and knowledge for practice

The internet is replete with information resources. They include bibliographic databases, journals, news services, government and quasi-governmental bodies, educational materials, research centres and projects, and mailing lists.[4] Some of the *bibliographic databases* are subscription-based. Examples of such services are those run by the National Children's Bureau (http://www. childdata.org.uk/) and The Centre for Policy on Ageing (http://www.cpa. org.uk/ageinfo/ageinfo2.html). With access to university libraries there are now gateways to a range of databases that cover many hundreds of journals through a single search. This is unfortunately rarely available to practitioners within agencies. An important exception is the Social Care Online free database accessible through the Social Care Institute for Excellence (SCIE). It is weighted to UK books, journal articles, and reports. The search system is user-friendly. However, it will not give access to the full text of articles. Users can register and receive email alerts of additions in their area of specialism. The SCIE website has links to other databases in the fields of alcohol and drug misuse, black and minority ethnic people, children and young people, health and social care, learning disabilities, mental health, older people, wider social policy and the social sciences.

---

[4] See Chapter 6 for further discussion of these

A further important database is Intute, launched in 2006 (http://www. intute.ac.uk/). This is a free online service providing access to the web resources for education and research, through a consortium of seven major UK universities. The database contains more than 110,000 records which have been selected and evaluated by subject specialists. The database can be searched or browsed by subject areas. Within the social sciences section is a list of 23 social welfare topics. Users can register their own MyIntute account to save search results, and gain email alerts. The entries in the social welfare section are different from the databases mentioned so far, in that the links are to a wide variety of documents, organisations and legislation, rather than to abstracts of research papers. In this respect it may be of more everyday value to social worker than mainstream databases.

The SCIE site is, at the time of writing, the most important UK social care site for access to wide ranging and free information. SCIE is an independent charity, funded by the Department of Health and the devolved administrations in Wales and Northern Ireland. The corresponding, though rather different, body in Scotland is The Institute for Research and Innovation in Social Services (IRISS: (http://www.iriss.org.uk/)). SCIE aims to identify and disseminate the knowledge base for good practice in all aspects of social care for children and adults throughout the United Kingdom. Their website reasonably claims that SCIE has developed a number of methodological approaches that reflect the kind of knowledge available in social care, including systematic mapping, systematic knowledge reviews, and user and carer involvement in systematic reviews. They may well develop guidelines for practice surveys, methods of rapid evidence assessment, a tool for kite-marking good practice, and a new approach to economic evaluation. The extensive information is of interest to those working in social work and social care research, and also to students, practitioners, and people who use services. IRISS has a valuable additional feature, in the regular posting of blogs, typically in the form of interviews about key themes and developments (see 'Taking it Further' at the end of this chapter).

It is also worth spending time exploring the work of the Centre of Excellence in Interdisciplinary Mental Health. It is a project funded by the Higher Education Funding Council for England that worked with practitioners, students, academics and service users and carers to create a range of text and videobased resources. All the resources created over the five-year period are freely accessible. The approach of the Centre has been to create 'granular' resources using ICT to provide service users with 'a voice' to express their experiences with the aim of influencing the development of effective interdisciplinary teaching, training and practice. Start with an overview of the Centre's resources (http://www.ceimh.bham.ac.uk/downloads/atoz.shtml) and move on to access the service user and carer digital stories: (http://www.ceimh.bham.ac.uk/tv/DigitalStoriesIntro.shtml).

A different category of information resources is that provided through mailing lists and news services. We have hinted at these already, in referring to the facility for regular mailings from most of the main database sites. The general distinction between a news service and a mailing list is that the latter allows a moderate degree of network exchange in response to news mailings. One of the most diverse, reliable and extensive lists, independent of any parent database, is available through the regular e-bulletin from SWAP, the Social Policy and Social Work subject centre (http://www.swap.ac.uk/). While this is primarily targeted at university students and teachers, and has a pedagogic thrust, there is much of value for practitioners via the e-bulletin and newsletter.

Understanding knowledge and evidence

We noted that the SCIE site has a wide range of research-based knowledge downloadable without charge. This is perhaps the most extensive social work and social care site of its kind in the world. While relatively straight-forward in ICT terms (there are minimal facilities for interaction with the site), the volume and accessibility of material on the site are too easily undervalued. It is also the location for one of the few social-work-tailored sets of guidance on the varied possibilities for systematic review, scoping studies and systematic mapping of knowledge, which could with profit be adopted by agency staff engaged in reviewing text resources. SCIE acknowledges its debt to the ePPI Centre (http://eppi.ioe.ac.uk), based within the Institute for Education at the University of London. The ePPI Centre stresses the involvement of users in the review process, thus illus-trating ways in which values at the heart of social work and cognate profes-sions have become part of some ICT initiatives.

> A particular aim of the ePPI-Centre is to explore the perspectives and partici-pation of those people who are, or represent, people receiving a service or who are affected by the service in some other way. This might include: patients in a clinical encounter; students in a classroom; people receiving, missing or avoiding health promotion interventions; or students and parents in relation to an education policy. (ePPI-Centre, 2010)

Perhaps the main form taken by sites providing knowledge and evidence for social work is research reports and digests. The simplest version of these consists of research text in its original or summary form being available for download, as on the SCIE site, university research units, or funding agencies such as the Joseph Rowntree Foundation (http://www.jrf.org.uk/). The Joseph Rowntree 'Research Findings' series often has been imitated but rarely bettered. Several of the reviews in the ePPI Centre 'knowledge library' also are relevant to social work practice.

A step on from this is found in sites that aim to develop practice application from research. The 'Research in Practice' e-learning site, for example, offers interactive research quizzes on such topics as educating difficult adolescents, or advocacy and participation. The site also includes a register of researchers – a database that holds contact details for researchers whose work may be of interest to children's services professionals, together with a list of their research interests and methods, current research projects and key publications.

Another variant on straight 'evidence' or 'knowledge' can be found in outlets that also focus on the development of skills for doing research. For example, the JISCmail social work lists referred to when we discuss networking below, include lists for those interested in fields such as grounded theory or narrative methods in practice and research. The growth of online books is another source of research methods skills that is increasingly available without charge or membership, and therefore not always restricted to those with a university connection.[5] Discussion lists, to which we refer below in the context of networking, sometimes afford knowledge development of this order, as for example the discussion list of the American Evaluation Association, and discussion lists set up for interest groups in the membership of the Society for Social Work and Research in the USA (http://www.sswr.org/). Participants in the international field of evidence-based policy and practice were among the early entrants in the field of collating resources for evidence and knowledge. For instance, the Evidence Network website offers an information resource provided by the Centre for Evidence & Policy at King's College London. The Evidence Network was founded in 2001 and has in view anyone concerned with evidence-based policy and practice in the broad field of social and public policy. The Network monitors news and events in the evidence-based policy and practice world, provides access to information resources in social and public policy, and acts as a gateway to the relevant literature (http://www.kcl.ac.uk/

---

[5] See for example the extensive list of links to such material in the evaluation field provided by the American Evaluation Association at http://www.eval.org/Resources/onlinehbtxt.asp.

schools/sspp/interdisciplinary/evidence/). In a similar intellectual context, the Campbell Collaboration (often referred to as C2) is an international research network that produces systematic reviews of the effects of social interventions. Campbell is based on voluntary cooperation among researchers of a variety of backgrounds. Social Welfare is one of its five coordinating groups (http://camp.ostfold.net/social_welfare/index.php). There are almost 30 completed reviews that can be accessed from the Campbell home site.

Practice skills

The proportion of social workers who will desire to gain or enhance research skills will almost certainly be outnumbered by those who wish to draw on ICT resources to develop their practice skills. Yet the resources that are so far available are probably less in both volume and usefulness than ICT-based research skills. Take, for example, the *Disability Handbook* produced in the UK by the Department for Work and Pensions. It is aimed at staff adjudicating claims for benefits, and is little more than a text of procedures online (http://www.dwp.gov.uk/docs/dla.pdf).

Rather better for our purposes is the material in another central government department, the Department of Health, that has responsibility for services for adults. The main site has a link to a relatively extensive care network. While it shares an almost inevitable tendency for central government sponsored sites to be less critical of service provision, the DH Care Networks team helpfully addresses, at the time of writing, a range of interesting and valuable resources around integration and whole system reform, housing with care, assistive technology and partnership working. Among the elements that have particular value as a source of practice skill development are the networks that address the personalisation agenda, prevention and intervention, and integrated care.[6] They go beyond a mere data deposit function, and include helpful interactive aspects, such as key messages, self-assessment quizzes, linked podcasts, film clips and good practice examples.

Networking

In moving through the various forms of knowledge-learning we have shifted from the most passive to more active forms of engaging with ICT. One of the oldest forms of networking is that provided through

---

[6]http://www.dhcarenetworks.org.uk/ See Chapter Five for further reference to service development through ICT resources.

discussion lists. The best starting point to discover what lists are available in the broad social work field is the National Academic Mailing List Service, known as JISCmail. While once more this is a service for the university and research communities, it hosts the largest assembly of practice-related lists and is free (http://jisc.ac.uk). There are over 60 lists under 'social work'. By way of illustration there are lists on alcohol misuse, adult protection, Child and Adolescent Mental Health Service (CAMHS), a carer forum, a child participation network, and anti-racism. For practitioners who wish to go one step further and set up their own list, there are full details on the JISCmail site on how to do so. Outside the JISC service, one of the most intelligent, rich, diverse and engaging lists is that provided through the American Evaluation Association.[7] It is specialist in purpose, of course, but quite outstanding, and open to non-members. The National Association of Social Workers (NASW) in the USA has a range of member blog resources, in the areas of advocacy, practice specialties, and media news (http://www.socialworkblog.org/). NASW also hosts scheduled weekly real-time chats and bulletin boards on a range of topics, for which social work members can sign up. The NASW site announces, 'we're here to offer you an opportunity to meet with colleagues in real-time chat rooms to learn, share ideas and build a network of social workers you can count on whenever you need support' (http://www.socialworkchat.org/). Opportunities also exist for members to participate in the monthly one-hour teleconferences. These are practice-oriented, covering such topics as the assessment and support of coping skills for cancer-related anxiety and depression.

One approach to capitalising on networks that is believed by several people to have promise for social work practitioners is through Communities of Practice (CoP). The interest for us is where such communities operate online through virtual communities. In some ways a CoP is very much like an informal network. Their distinctive nature lies in when such communities develop – or are initiated – with a focus on a particular domain of knowledge and the purpose of gaining knowledge and expertise through their continuing interaction. It is difficult to recall that the general access to email is still much less than 20 years old at the time of writing. The impact of the advent of email on facilitating international networking in the social work community is hard to reimagine.

Proponents of virtual CoPs believe that such communities 'can be an effective mechanism for balancing the shortage of available evidence and

---

[7]EVALTAK can be joined from http://www.aime.ua.edu/cgi-bin/wa?SUBED1=evaltalk&A=1.

the development of actionable knowledge or practice' (Cook-Craig and Sabah, 2009: 727). These authors proceed to say that the communities:

> [P]rovide a new, geographically unbounded opportunity to create, verify, store and diffuse knowledge in the profession ... [they] also offer an opportunity for practitioners to develop weak ties ... [and] gain new knowledge and ways of practice *across* organisations and disciplines. (2009: 728)

Without wishing to discourage practitioner engagement with CoP opportunities, several cautions need bearing in mind. LaMendola and colleagues (2009) report a small but careful research study from which they conclude – in line with other studies – that such networks are likely to 'function regardless of media, meaning that such communities can be supported by, but are not necessarily an effect of, communication technology employment itself' (2009: 721). Their results also indicated that practitioners viewed online contact as a supplement to face-to-face contact, and that the most beneficial activities were those that were face-to-face. This conclusion echoes the results of a study, also in Scotland, of a network of social workers engaged in practitioner research, and supported by staff from a university social work programme through a mix of face-to-face and email contacts (Lunt et al., 2009).

ICT as Practice

We remarked earlier that an additional way of viewing ICT within social work is to express it as part and parcel of direct practice – of assessment, planning, intervention, recording, reviewing or evaluating. For example, in the health field 'telemedicine' has been prominent for some time. The expression 'telesocialwork' has not yet surfaced, but the idea of telecare *is* beginning to figure. For example, the Telecare Learning and Improvement Network is the national network supporting local service redesign through the application of telecare and telehealth to aid the delivery of housing, health, social care and support services for older and vulnerable people (http://www.dhcarenetworks.org.uk/IndependentLivingChoices/Telecare/). Telecare is a broad term which encompasses a wide range of technologies with remote monitoring that can support people to remain independent and potentially reduce the frequency of hospital and care home admissions. A major evaluation of telecare and telehealth is due to report in 2011. Grand predictions are sometimes made for these developments.

Robots, domestic appliances that could think for themselves, voice activated lights, wireless communicators – all 20th century sci-fi images of what life would be now. These are the sorts of images that our now elderly population grew up with and, for them at least, much of it is becoming a reality. (Mickel and Miskelly, 2009)

A safer guide can be found in Beech and Roberts' briefing (2008) on *assistive technology* for older people. We quoted their conclusions regarding benefits of assistive technology claimed by those who use such services in the previous chapter. They suggest that types of assistive technology can be categorised or grouped according to their role:

- supportive technologies for helping individuals perform tasks that they may find difficult (for example, video entry systems, and medication reminder units);
- detection and reaction (responsive) technologies to help individuals manage risks and raise alarms (for example, unburned gas detectors and panic buttons/pendants);
- prediction and intervention (preventive) technologies to help prevent dangerous situations and, again, to raise alarms (for example, falls predictors, monitors for assessing physiological symptoms, room occupancy monitors).

Assistive technology and telecare have thus far been developed in the fields of health and services for older people. A development that has different applications is that of *online counselling*. Services of this nature have developed in growing numbers in the independent sector and, in the UK at least, have stemmed from the counselling field rather than the mainstream social work sector. According to advocates of this development, it includes online support groups, counselling via webcam, and asynchronous online counselling (Murphy et al., 2009). There is a UK Association for Counselling and Therapy Online, made up of psychological therapists.

Due to the somewhat evangelistic nature of the online counselling and therapy movement, claims to online success (or, in Murphy and colleagues' terms, equal levels of success) should be treated with some caution. For example, there is no attention to understanding the ways that practice and technology mediate one another.

The mediation of technology through practice

The work of a number of social work researchers has led them to question the conclusion that technology determines what social workers do. Research with social workers in Belgium concludes as follows:

The mutual opposition of technology and social services is limited … Computerization is a part of structures,[8] having influences and being influenced by human workers or human actions. (Laurent, 2008: 383)

It follows that 'Workers can also manifest strategic attitudes of resistance … They always have the possibilities of playing with the rules' (p. 383). Pithouse and colleagues reach a similar conclusion about IT programmes in social work when they refer to 'the potential for moderation and "work-arounds" by staff in order to win some advantage' (Pithouse et al., 2009: 604). Shaw and Clayden refer to the presence of tactics to defend service users, whereby service users were deliberately not informed about technology innovations, online forms were adapted 'on the hoof', and when the scheme was seen as requiring unrealistic expectations it was soft-pedalled at local level (Shaw and Clayden, 2009).

Example 4.1 gives a synopsis of the UK government's introduction of an approach to social work with children that places ICT at the heart of practice, and presents some points from an evaluation of the system. The balance of the evaluation findings were, in this instance, critical. But they help to illustrate how the mutual mediation of practice and technology takes place in local services.

Example 4.1   The Integrated Children's System

The Integrated Children's System (ICS) is a government-led initiative from London and Cardiff, and is part of a wider package of developments for children's services, designed to promote effective services for children and families in England and Wales. It aims to help them do this 'in a systematic manner, and to enable practitioners and managers to collect and use information systematically, efficiently and effectively' (Department for Children, 2009a). The government laid out the key elements of ICS as:

- an understanding of social work as consisting of assessment, planning, intervention and review;
- a set of data requirements providing common information from one locality to the other about children and families;
- a set of 'exemplar' formats for social work practitioners and other agencies, which form the basis for an e-social care record.

(Continued)

---

[8]The writer is drawing on the work of the sociologist Anthony Giddens on structuration.

(Continued)

A national evaluation of the ICS drew five conclusions about the relationship between social work practice and technology (Shaw and Clayden, 2009).

A. The ICS actively shaped practice. It:

    1 brought issues into focus, rendered social work visible, but served to partialise practice in a way that made it difficult to see the whole story;

    2 challenged practitioners to consider what counted as 'important' or 'serious' evidence and what counted as less 'serious' or weighty.

    3 unhelpfully 'fixed' the character of social work evidence;

    4 'pre-coded' some aspects of practice and left others 'open-ended';

    5 changed some language forms of social work to information terms.

B. ICS helped to disentangle, and bring into focus and clarify, though not solve, issues that had been there previously but had been rendered less visible by existing recording and practice systems.

C. The ICS made social work more visible, but it was a certain kind of visibility – a performance culture visibility.

D. The ICS distanced the service user.

    1 It was *overwhelming for service users* to cope with.

    2 The *language* used in the forms was difficult to understand.

    3 The *volume and density of information* required from the exemplars was seen as intrusive.

E. It led to new forms of discretion by practitioners as they found ways of working with the ICS at a local level.

Practitioners need not draw wholly negative conclusions from such research. Social workers should be neither optimists nor 'doomsayers' regarding technology. But it does oblige us to think critically about each aspect of social work practice. Take recording as an example. An argument that, even at this distance in time, remains striking was made by the influential early sociologist, Ernest Burgess at Chicago.[9] The main case he develops is about the potential but largely unrealised value of agency case records, especially regarding families (Burgess, 1923). 'What should social case records contain to be useful for sociological interpretation? They

---

[9]There have been major developments in the field of library studies in digitisation. One result has been the steady growth in the availability for downloading of formerly difficult to trace journal holdings. The Burgess articles cited in this chapter can all be downloaded from JSTOR: 'JSTOR is a not-for-profit organisation that aims to preserve a record of scholarship for posterity and to advance research and teaching in cost-effective ways'. Access is via a licence fee. http://www.jstor.org/.

should contain what will render them valuable for social case work, that and no more. This answer will, I know, perplex and astonish many social workers and sociologists' (Burgess, 1928: 524).

His specific proposal is enticing:

> My proposal is actually quite simple and I think, entirely feasible and reasonable, in spite of the fact that I do not anticipate its immediate and general adoption. It is to enter into the case record statements made by all persons visited in nearly as humanly possible the language which they used. (Burgess, 1927: 192)

Quoting the prominent nineteenth-century British housing reformer, Octavia Hill, he laments

> Existing case records seldom, or never, picture people in the language of Octavia Hill, with their 'passions, hopes, and history' or their 'temptations', or 'the little scheme they have made of their lives, or would make if they had encouragement'. The characters in case records do not move, and act, and have their being as persons. They are depersonalized, they become Robots, or mere cases undifferentiated except by the recurring problems they present. (Burgess, 1928: 526–7)

Why refer to writing nine decades old in the context of ICT? Because the more severe criticisms of ICS records as made by social workers in the study we have summarised were to the effect that the possibility of a 'narrative', of the kind Burgess would have recognised, was lost in the detailed compartmentalising that took place in the 'Exemplar' records. There are forms of readily available technology, such as voice recognition software, that would seem to yield opportunities for ways of recording that are in closer harmony with good practice than the extended apparatus of the ICS. Burgess' remarks also confront social workers of today as of years-past Chicago with the question of whether all ways of recording move too readily to professional accounts at the expense of hearing the voice of service users.

Challenges and opportunities

Skills, interest, critical awareness, perceived fit between agency and service user needs, and resource accessibility are all essential if practitioners are to engage with the challenges and opportunities presented by developments in ICT. They overlap. Take resources and skills. We mentioned earlier the comments of social workers in an evaluation of a practitioner research network. The final report concluded that practitioner research supported at agency level is likely to focus attention on the general adequacy of agency-wide IT systems and the way this is complicated by practitioners' acknowledged limitations in ICT skills.

'I suppose that would have been helpful to have had that conversation quite early on with [agency] managers – 'what support can we get in terms of technology?'... I think ... the tutors were talking about quite expensive technology that we didn't have a budget for in our projects'. (Alan)

While this was nowhere expressed as a 'heavy' criticism, it was perhaps compounded by limited IT skills among some cohort members. 'The IT bit of it ... was quite a challenge for me'. 'I get really confused with the editing software with these machines.' (Lunt et al., 2009: 36)

There is probably sufficient recurrent anecdotal evidence to suggest that inter- and even intra-agency variations in access to hardware and software militate against a community of exchange within social work.

Resource constraints are also present in the inadequate access practitioners have to subscription-based ICT provision. This is probably due to a mixture of limited professional development budgets, a strategy of favouring composite subscription sites such as Research in Practice, and a preference for ready-processed materials that prescribe 'good practice' over 'raw' materials that call for critical reflection and transfer of learning.

Yet a deficit analysis is probably not sufficient to account for troubles on the ICT front. For example, there have been repeated, if sometimes disputed, claims that ICT developments lead to a substantial increase in the time social workers spend at their screens, to the detriment of face-to-face direct practice (e.g., SCIE, 2006; Shaw and Clayden, 2009). There are also the deep-seated concerns outlined in this chapter about a lack of 'fit' between forms of ICT as they are manifested in policy innovations in social work and social care, and practice principles and values. Questions of practice ethics, quality control and data security can each be added to this list.

Yet iconoclasm is not an option. It is widely accepted, for example, that new media technologies have facilitated social activism and enhanced the effectiveness of civil society organisations in their work. Over the years there have been successful examples of civil society organising, using ICTs, to achieve results. Some of the notable ones in this class include the Seattle protests against the World Trade Organization (WTO) during its 1999 ministerial meeting; the defeat of the coup against Boris Yeltsin in 1991, which was foiled largely due to the civil society organisations' efforts at sending out numerous emails that facilitated mobilisation of opposition against the coup; the ousting of Milošević in former Yugoslavia; and the demonstrations that rocked Iran following its presidential election in 2009.

What should practitioners do? Practitioners' action is likely to be most effective when their engagement is at a community level and takes a variety of forms (see Laurent, 2008).

- *Regional or national collaboration*. In the UK, for example, there are likely to be ICT interests at the level of Scotland, Wales, Northern Ireland, and the English regions. Such platforms could have a voice as intermediaries between social workers and public authorities and computer companies. They could also press for a more equal and extensive investment in subscription-based resources, and exemplify the values of existing resources, including those free at the point of use.
- *Participatory design* of ICT packages for social work. Policy innovations that involve organisations where knowledge workers are the agents of service delivery are likely to raise substantial and relatively enduring challenges to 'understand the social relations of the workplace and their implications for systems design' (Hartswood et al., 2002: 10). Yet design developments typically exclude practitioners, and are premised on the false assumption that the only relevant kinds of knowledge for such development are those of technology and management.
- *Communities of practice*. While virtual CoPs are unlikely to offer a panacea, staying alert to existing and emerging communities could allow social workers, to echo Cook-Craig and Sabah (2009), to create, assess, store and diffuse knowledge in the profession, and offer an opportunity for practitioners to develop otherwise weak ties through gaining new knowledge and ways of practice *across* organisations and disciplines. Take, for example, the huge amount of digitisation that is happening through libraries and elsewhere. This offers opportunities to social workers to press for archiving of recent and earlier parts of the profession's heritage (cf. Daly and Ballantyne, 2009). On a different front, CoPs, perhaps through professional associations, could take a view as to whether all practitioners should be enabled to achieve European Computer Driving Licence skills levels.

The practitioner-level themes of this chapter have obvious connections with ICT at service and agency levels and we turn to these in the next chapter.

Taking it further

Exercise 4.1: Social workers as knowledge workers

The idea that social workers are 'knowledge workers' is helpful in developing a reflective understanding of the implications of how ICT is embedded in everyday practice, and in connecting developments in social work to those in other comparable occupations and professions. Search for a useful discussion of the general idea, which may include

(Continued)

(Continued)

a Wikipedia entry if it exists. For a critical review of debates see the article by Darr and Warhurst (2008). Check by internet search if there have been recent applications of the idea directly to social work.

Exercise 4.2: Building understanding and knowledge

Go to the store of podcasts on the IRISS site at http://www.iriss.org. uk/rss/podcast/sieswe.xml. Select one of interest and relevance to this chapter. After listening, check out what relevant evidence you can find from any of the ICT resources mentioned in this chapter.

5

ICT and Social Work Agencies

In Chapter 2 we considered how ICTs have become an integral part of the basic elements of social work practice: in social work assessments, case recording, and so on. In doing so we reported on the claims made for the use of ICTs in these areas, but refrained from discussing in any depth the emerging critique of the ways in which social work practice may be changing as a result. In Chapters 3 and 4 we looked at the impact on service users and on social workers of the increasing use of ICTs and included some of this critique. In the current chapter it is time to draw this material together and to consider ICT use at the level of social work agencies, concentrating on the use of electronic databases for various kinds of record keeping.

In this chapter we will first highlight some of the commonly held concerns, or objections, to the use of ICT by social work agencies and their partners. We will then explore these concerns in relation to three real-world examples of the use of ICT in social work agencies: the use of electronic assessment tools; the Integrated Children's System; and ContactPoint. In considering these examples, our aim will be to assess the validity of the criticisms presented in the early part of the chapter and, where relevant, to try to identify the potential for best practice in the use of ICT by social work agencies.

Parts of this chapter are critical in tone. These reflect reservations that arise from our research and practice experience. However, we are not doomsayers regarding technology. Our purpose in writing in this way is to provide a basis to engage with the exercise at the end of the chapter, that orients you to positive lesson-learning.

Concerns and Objections

Databases, information, and the loss of narrative

The information on computer databases is usually entered and stored in relatively small units that can be easily manipulated. Online forms for data entry often have 'radio buttons', or 'drop-down menus' that pre-define the choices that users can make. When such forms have 'free-text' fields these are usually restricted in size, with a limit on how much text can be entered. Once entered, individual pieces of 'information' can be reorganised and the relationships between them can be changed.

Nigel Parton (2008b) argues that as social workers use database systems for recording their work, their knowledge is transformed. Knowledge that was 'social' and 'relational' becomes fragmented into items of information. Such information may become stripped of its context.

> At the same time, knowledge which cannot be squeezed into the required format disappears or gets lost. This has particular implications for the way in which identities are constructed and the type of human experience which can be represented. Stories of violence, pain and social deprivation can only be told within the required parameters to the point that they may not be stories at all. (Parton, 2008b: 262)

The concern about using ICT in this way is that it disrupts the construction of the kind of narratives about service users and their situations that enable professionals to make sense of their work (Hall, 1997). Sue White and colleagues (White et al., 2009) provide an illustration of this kind of disruption in relation to the introduction in England of the electronic Common Assessment Framework (eCAF), and we will examine this later in relation to electronic assessment tools. Our aim in this chapter is to assess the seriousness of this concern and to consider what it may mean for best practice.

The significance of relationships in social work

The argument that relationships are central to social work practice is not a new one, but it has been persuasively restated recently by Wilson and colleagues (2008). The professional relationship with the service user can be seen as 'the medium through which the practitioner can engage with and intervene in the complexity of an individual's internal and external worlds' (Wilson et al., 2008: 7). Such helping relationships are complex and unique. Making them work effectively is a skilled task which requires high quality face-to-face supervision, and arguably not the kind of computerised 'performance management' to which social workers are increasingly subject.

The concern is that the integration of ICT systems into social work makes it more difficult to form helping relationships. Two factors may be at play here. First, there is the priority given to 'computer work' over face-to-face work with service users. Paul Garrett (2005) begins an article about social work's 'electronic turn' by reflecting on the imagery used in a job advert from 2004. Here the largest element of the picture was a computer, with a female worker sitting and using a keyboard. In fact, social workers told the Social Work Task Force that bureaucratic IT systems all too frequently act as a barrier to good practice (Social Work Taskforce, 2009b). As Howe (1996) argued some years ago, social work has become centred on gathering information so as to categorise services users (for example, high or low risk; moderate or critical needs) rather than on forming relationships with people so as to understand the causes of their difficulties in their social context. The concern is that the introduction of ICT has accelerated the trend. Second, and as we have seen, there is the concern that computerised recording systems cannot easily reflect the significant subtleties of helping relationships. We will assess these concerns in relation to the examples later in the chapter.

Managerialism and surveillance of staff

As we saw in Chapter 2, the introduction of ICTs into social work was strongly linked to the New Labour government's modernising agenda for e-government, and to management's demand for accountability (Sapey, 1997). Despite widespread acceptance of legitimate managerial interests in the use of ICTs, there has always been concern about the degree to which these interests all too easily outweigh those of staff and service users. Research into the parallel field of social security systems in 13 countries demonstrates the widespread tendency for management interests to dominate ICT systems, resulting not in empowered staff and claimants but in increased management control over them (Henman and Adler, 2003). There is concern that this is also happening in social work. Garrett (2005) points to increasing ICT-enabled management surveillance of staff in a number of different areas of social work.

Civil liberties, privacy and data protection

The rapid development of electronic databases over recent years has led to concerns about the growth of the 'surveillance society' and the impact on privacy, civil liberties and human rights (Ball et al., 2006). The debate is about how to uphold privacy and civil liberties whilst at the same time safeguarding national security, fighting crime and protecting children by collecting increased amounts of data. Several serious breaches of UK government data security have been reported: the Ministry of Defence lost 69 laptops including army recruits' personal details and HM Revenue & Customs lost the entire records of 25 million child benefit claimants (Sweney, 2009). In an influential report, the civil liberties group, the Joseph Rowntree Reform Trust (JRRT), assessed 46 databases across the major government departments and found that:

- A quarter of the public-sector databases reviewed are almost certainly illegal under human rights or data protection law; they should be scrapped or substantially redesigned.
- More than half have significant problems with privacy or effectiveness and could fall foul of a legal challenge.
- Fewer than 15% of the public databases assessed in this report are effective, proportionate and necessary, with a proper legal basis for any privacy intrusions (Anderson et al., 2009).

Amongst those coded 'red' for danger by the JRRT are the ContactPoint database and the electronic Common Assessment Framework. We will examine these concerns in more detail later.

Making ICT work

Somewhat ironically, in view of the previous concerns about privacy, there are concerns about whether complex ICT systems can actually be made to function properly. Critics insist that the government has a very poor track record with ICT projects, with the JRRT report cited above claiming that 'only about 30% of government IT projects succeed' (Anderson et al., 2009). We have already noted that social workers told the 2009 Social Work Taskforce that bureaucratic ICT systems all too frequently act as a barrier to good practice (Social Work Taskforce, 2009b). A significant part of this complaint was simply about technical problems: for example, systems that crash, or lock users out unexpectedly. But some were about the impact of ICT systems on direct practice.

In what follows we will use three real-world examples – the use of 'electronic' assessment tools; the Integrated Children's System; and ContactPoint – to explore the relevance of these concerns. An optimistic reading of the value of this analysis stems from research which suggests that students, having developed critical thinking during their social work degree studies, with increased confidence apply this critique to ICT (Nix, 2010). In some instances students are starting to think through what would make the systems perform better to reflect more closely their practice needs. Some are prepared to challenge the system, speak to the IT departments about needed improvements, and support colleagues in using systems, especially when they perceive that failure to do so might result in information being lost or not recorded.

'Electronic' Assessments

In recent years there has been a steady increase in the mandatory use of 'structured' assessment tools. Such tools provide a national framework for gathering information and for decision making. Examples include:

- ASSET for the assessment of young people who have offended (Youth Justice Board, 2006);
- the Framework for Assessment of Children in Needs and their Families (FFA) (Department of Health, 2000);
- the Common Assessment Framework (CAF) (Department for Children, 2009e).

Two of the above, and some similar assessment tools, began life as paper forms. More recently, electronic versions have been introduced, with information being entered into databases for sharing between professionals, sometimes in other agencies. We will consider some of the wider issues that emerge from using databases in the following section, using the example of the Integrated Children's System. But for now the focus is on assessment practice in agencies that use standardised, electronic assessment tools. It should be acknowledged that some of the issues that are considered here were relevant even when these assessments were being completed on paper. But we will see how they are brought more sharply into focus in the electronic versions.

We should note that standardised, electronic assessment tools are being introduced into many areas of social work, including adult services. For example, a Common Assessment Framework for Adults was being piloted during 2009 (Department of Health, 2009). However, development of the CAF in adult services is not so far advanced as the equivalent in children's services, where there is a body of emerging research evidence. In this section we will examine that evidence in relation to the development of the eCAF (the electronic version of the Common Assessment Framework).

1. Development of unborn baby, infant, child or young person

Identity, self-esteem, self-image and social presentation
Perceptions of self; knowledge of personal/family history; sense of belonging; experiences of discrimination due to race, religion, age, gender, sexuality and disability

Family and social relationships
Building stable relationships with family, peers and wider community; helping others; friendships; levels of association for negative relationships

Self-care skills and independence
Becoming independent; boundaries, rules, asking for help, decision making; changes to body; washing, dressing, feeding; positive separation from family

FIGURE 5.1   *Sub-domains in the CAF*

Record keeping and the eCAF

The CAF is designed for use by a range of child welfare professionals, with the specific aim of creating a 'common language' for assessment. The CAF consists of a standard form containing two substantive sections (whether as a Word template or online as 'eCAF'). The first section is a list of 'sub-domains' that are closely related to those in the Framework for Assessment. Workers are asked to enter information that is relevant to each sub-domain. A part of the form is reproduced as Figure 5.1, showing a few of the sub-domains.

The second section is more analytical. It requires the author to consider what changes are needed, what the aims of any work are, and how they can be achieved. This should lead to a list of agreed actions, and a process for reviewing progress. A part of this analytical section is reproduced as Figure 5.2.

Ethnographic research was undertaken during 2005–6, by Sue White and colleagues, in four local authorities that were amongst the first to implement the CAF (White et al., 2009). This shows how these forms may disrupt the use of the kinds of storied accounts of service users' lives that are typical of professional assessments. Specifically, there is no room for a

Conclusions, solutions and actions

Now the assessment is completed you need to record conclusions, solutions and actions. Work with the baby, child or young person and/or parent or carer, and take account of their ideas, solutions and goals.

What are your aims?*
(What are the key aims the child, young person and/or family would like to address?)

What are your conclusions?*
(What are the child/young person's/families strengths and resources, what are their needs – e.g., no additional needs, additional needs, complex needs, risk of harm to self or others?)

Strengths & resources:

Needs/worries:

What changes are wanted?*
(Include the child/young person's, parent/carer's and practitioner's views)

FIGURE 5.2   *Analysis in the CAF*

chronological perspective on developments in the family's story, nor on the involvement of professionals. Some of the workers interviewed during the study felt that, by removing any space for 'background' or 'family history' and starting with the list of domains, it was impossible to tell what the assessment was about. As a learning mentor in a primary school put it:

> 'You can't give your general history. There is nowhere where you can give background and that's so important I mean to me. If you. That's what people need to know. It's about the background and it goes straight into those, you know those boxes which … I mean all you've had up to there has been you know mother and father and siblings. But NO background on that child. And because of the what this particular pupil had witnessed prior to that had a massive effect on WHY he was like he is. And obviously without that information everybody's in the dark.' (White et al., 2009: 1206)

White and colleagues argue that the CAF is deliberately designed to force out narrative accounts of how we got to this point and to replace it with an analysis of 'strengths' and 'needs' that is 'evidence-based'. But their research demonstrates that workers find this very difficult. In fact White and colleagues provide evidence of workers finding ways of smuggling narrative accounts into the CAF forms, often preferring to use the open boxes in the 'analysis' section and to skip over some or all of the domains in the first section. Some even use 'copy' and 'paste' to repeat these narrative elements in various places where they may be relevant, presumably to help readers to find the crucial material amidst the disconnected elements of the assessment. The research shows that, in addition to the 'descriptive demands' placed on writers, the CAF also places 'interpretive demands' on readers who may struggle to discern what the case was 'really about'.

The CAF aims to standardise professional activity, with all child welfare professionals using the same framework and a 'common language' for assessment. However, White and colleagues report how many of the CAFs they examined had boxes that remained uncompleted. This might be because workers felt that they lacked the professional expertise in that area (for example, school teachers were reluctant to comment on parenting issues) or because they felt that some areas were not relevant to that family. There were also difficulties for some professionals in making judgements that were outside their usual knowledge and experience, for example about 'acceptable' or 'unacceptable' home conditions. And it was clear that, because the CAF is being used increasingly as a means of referral to another specialist agency, writers were presenting information 'in a manner designed to engage their interest and resources' (White et al., 2009: 1212). In short, White and colleagues conclude that, because of the continuing variety of professional backgrounds, remits and organisational purposes, there may be little that is 'common' about recording practice using the CAF.

Using the eCAF with service users

The ethic of the CAF is that it is consent-driven. Towards the end of the form there is space for the comments of children and young people and their parents and carers. They can also give consent to the CAF being shared with other, named, agencies, and are informed of circumstances in which information might be shared without their consent.

Research into the CAF in England showed that a sizeable minority of assessments (24 per cent) had no indication of agreement from adults and the majority had no indication of agreement from children (Pithouse et al., 2009). The researchers suggest that the CAF may have made adult service users more 'visible' than in the past, but that the limited involvement of children and young people is part of a wider pattern of professional culture. There is a suggestion that service users are less likely to be asked for their agreement or comments when the CAF is being used as a referral mechanism to, for example, the Education Welfare Office to investigate non-school attendance.

There are practical difficulties in using computer-based forms with service users. Typically, the work must first be entered into the computer system, then printed and taken,

> as a paper-based form to the adult and child for them to read, perhaps add text, or qualify, and finally endorse. The worker then needs to enter these changes into the electronic version in the office. Such a process of sharing and iteration inevitably prolongs an activity that has as its core aim a swift approach to information exchange. These transaction costs, together with the additional time involved in completing a CAF (it is likely that whatever was in place before the CAF would have been less elaborate and perhaps more informal), meant that staff across research sites tended to see the common assessment as creating more work for them (and necessarily away from clients), irrespective of and in some opposition to claims about new technological efficiencies. (Pithouse et al., 2009: 606)

Systems for remote working are now being developed so that workers may be able to use portable devices while visiting people in their own homes.

The Integrated Children's System

One of us was involved in an evaluation of the Integrated Children's System (ICS) that was carried out for the Department for Education and Skills and the Welsh Assembly Government (Bell et al., 2007). This section draws on that research. The research took place in councils that were piloting the ICS; two in England and two in Wales. The fieldwork was carried out from 2004 to 2006.

The ICS is a government-led system for delivering services to children in need in England and Wales. Local authorities have been required to have ICS systems in place since January 2007. According to the ICS website, it 'provides a conceptual framework, a method of practice and a business process to support practitioners and managers in undertaking the key tasks of assessment, planning, intervention and review' (Department for Children, 2009a).

The understanding of social work as a process of assessment, planning, intervention and review is central to the ICS. It provides a basis for managing 'workflow' that is analogous to workflow processes in industry and commerce. The idea of such a workflow is not a new one and, although there are some critical voices, it is widely accepted within social work. The novel feature of ICS is that the workflow system brings together service user records and management processes in a single electronic format that can be shared between localities. At the same time, it supports a particular model of assessment practice that was previously required by the Framework for Assessment (Department of Health, 2000) and is utilised in the eCAF. The ICS electronic record is based on a set of 'exemplar' formats, and individual local authorities are able to commission their own business solution from an ICT specialist.

ICS and the practice of social work recording

There is evidence from the evaluation of the ICS to show that social workers and their managers have concerns about the tendency of the ICS exemplars to break up the 'story' of the work in such a way as to make it difficult to understand the whole picture. This was a common complaint, well illustrated by this quotation from a research interview with a social worker:

> '…what is lost in that is the child. You don't get a picture of the child and their needs very succinctly. It is all lost in these questions and jargon. It is very difficult for another professional to read it and get a picture of the child.' (Shaw and Clayden, 2009: 19)

Social workers complained that the exemplars are simply too rigid and place undue constraints on their recording practice. Workers are sometimes required to choose between pre-defined options in drop-down boxes; to choose between 'yes' or 'no' tick box answers; and sometimes to respond to specific questions by typing inside text boxes, usually with limited numbers of permitted characters. These standardised options, and the required timescales, were said to provide too little flexibility to allow a detailed description of service users' needs. They promote the collection of repetitive and disconnected fragments rather than a coherent analysis of what should be done (Shaw et al., 2009b).

But the picture was not entirely negative. The study also produced evidence of social workers using the ICS to continue to produce what they felt were good records. Where this was happening, these workers were using their expertise to 'adapt' elements of the ICS, or they were responding to questions obliquely, in ways that seemed to them more relevant than a straightforward answer. One manager felt that an expert part of her role lay in advising social workers about which parts of the exemplars were not relevant in particular cases and could be left blank. In other words, some social workers had the confidence to respond to the ICS by varying what they recorded in response to how they understood the needs of the case, but they did not see the ICS as assisting this recording practice.

ICS and the impact on work with service users

There is evidence that the introduction of the ICS has affected the relationships between social workers and service users in several ways. First, the amount of time spent in front of the computer on 'data entry' increased from 15.5 to 27.1 per cent of all activities in the local authorities piloting the ICS. The social workers complained overwhelmingly that this significantly reduced the amount of time that they could spend with service users (Shaw et al., 2009b). Second, social workers felt that the exemplars were not user friendly. The volume and the density of the information required were seen as intrusive for families. As one social worker put it:

> 'I think we have to be careful really not to dehumanise the process,' cos this is people we are working with, and when you get into using language like that and 20 page long documents for a review of services you've been providing, you risk alienating people and leaving people feeling like they have been picked to pieces.' (Shaw and Clayden, 2009: 21)

It should be said that this is not what was intended. One of the stated aims of ICS is to make the process of providing social work services more open and understandable to families. But one of the effects of introducing 'a machine' into the process seems to be that of depersonalisation. Another of the social workers described the process of going back and forth between 'the machine' and the family as a loss of the sense of working together. This is not helped by some of the language used in the ICS exemplars. The term 'parenting capacity', for example, was felt to be difficult for parents of disabled children, or even offensive, insofar as it implies a possible deficit.

ICS and managerialism

We have already noted that the ICS has multiple policy objectives. Those most closely associated with a managerial agenda include: increasing accountability; transparency; delivering better management; and standardising good practice.

The ICS gives team leaders easy access to all the recording completed by social workers in their team (although technical problems may be a limitation – see below). There is no hiding place for poor or incomplete recording. The regulation of practitioners is much easier than it was before the ICS – and elements of it can even be automated using pre-programmed messages to prompt workers for overdue reviews and so on. This functionality is deliberate, and was designed into the ICS. A technical report for the DfES puts it like this:

> Essentially, the IT system forces users to follow best practice guidelines by, for example, automatically creating a review of a plan after a fixed time period, or initiating a core assessment if certain criteria are met. (Cleaver, 2005: 5)

Note the use of the word 'forces'. The term suggests that technology has the capacity to 'discipline' the user. There is a longstanding argument that ICT designers are able to 'configure the user' by determining exactly how users can interact with the software (Woolgar, 1991). Many social workers in the ICS study experienced this as deskilling and demoralising. They felt that the exemplars failed to ask questions that were relevant to some children, whilst asking of others questions that were irrelevant. They saw the separation of complex, interconnected material into discrete data entry fields as unhelpful (Bell et al., 2007). Yet in the ICS study there are clear examples of how social workers and their managers find ways to resist and to work around the discipline of the ICS, where they experienced this as running counter to good practice. The irony is that the ICS designers and the practitioners are both acting in the name of 'good practice'.

Our argument is that this shared aim of good practice offers some hope in what has otherwise been a fairly negative evaluation of the ICS. Social workers did not altogether lose their autonomy when using the ICS, but were able to some extent to vary what they recorded and how they practised. Indeed, one team leader argued that it was the quality of individual practitioners that was the key to good practice, rather than prescriptive exemplars:

> 'My own view is that the assessment could be much less prescriptive because ultimately at the end of the day it's about professional practice, it's about training and development and it's about making sure that that equips us to do the job ... unless you've got that level of professional expertise, it doesn't matter how many questions a piece of paper asks, you're never going to get the quality of work.' (Shaw et al., 2009a: 392)

One possible conclusion is that good practice in the use of ICT requires social workers, their managers and the policymakers to resolve questions about how all parties can contribute effectively to the design and development of ICT systems. But we suspect that this may be placing too much faith in the process of rational policy development. It seems more likely that IT systems will continue to be an uneasy fit with social work practices, and that social workers will respond by 'muddling through' – subtly subverting some elements of the system, and recreating others as they go. Our emphasis is not so much on how to design ICT systems that are social work friendly, worthy though that objective may be, but on how to nurture best social work practice in contexts that must necessarily incorporate imperfect ICT systems.

Making the ICS work

There is no doubt that there were significant technical problems with the introduction of the ICS. Users reported problems with 'complex logging on procedures, difficulties entering data, finding data located on different screens, reading screens that flickered or were too small, crashing systems and remote access. Users ... were unable to scan in letters and reports and were unable to sign off documents or transfer data securely by remote means' (Shaw et al., 2009b: 621). What has been at issue is the extent to which these can be seen as 'teething problems' and limited to the pilot sites. Clearly this question cannot be resolved using the data from the study, because this was limited to the pilot sites. However, it seems reasonable to conclude that we should not underestimate the technical difficulties of delivering new IT 'solutions'. Experience suggests that the amount of time taken to bed-in new systems is often longer than anticipated, and that the cost and the disruption caused are often underestimated.

The ICS and good practice in social work

At the beginning of the chapter we listed some of the general concerns about using ICT in social work. With the exception perhaps of concerns about civil liberties, each of these concerns is reflected in the data from the evaluation of ICS that we have referred to (Bell et al., 2007). However, the data does not point entirely in one direction. At the same time as there is evidence of dissatisfaction with the restrictions of the ICS exemplars, there is also evidence that some social workers are finding creative 'work-arounds', and that some managers are encouraging them in this. In other words, the development of ICS is experienced not only as imposing limits on professional discretion but, paradoxically, as opening up new areas in which it can operate.

We should also acknowledge that, by focusing on the concerns listed at the beginning of the chapter, we have not presented the more positive aspects of the study – limited though these were. Social workers have a strong commitment to the aims of the ICS. The ability to communicate a detailed picture of the child and the family across agencies electronically is seen as highly desirable. The need for accountability through record keeping is also widely accepted. But the overall conclusion of the study was that the ICS, as then constituted, was not able to deliver these aims. Since then, the Social Work Taskforce has drawn attention to some of these concerns. In its final report the Taskforce details some of the changes that are needed:

- simplification of the national specifications for ICS
- clarification that local authorities are responsible for the quality and usability of their IT, and for ensuring that it supports effective professional practice
- support to authorities in making local decisions about the future of their ICS systems, including: tools for assessing and improving usability; and guidance about how simplifications can be introduced whilst protecting the integrity of the system and continuing to support social workers to operate within the legal framework. (Social Work Taskforce, 2009a)

ContactPoint

ContactPoint is a national database for England whose legal basis rested in The Children Act 2004 and The Children Act 2004 Information Databases (England) Regulations 2007. We noted in Chapter 2 that one of the first acts of the new UK coalition government in May 2010 was to signal that

ContactPoint would be scrapped. However, we are using it as a peg to introduce themes and issues that will certainly recur in successor initiatives in the UK and in other countries. The official position was that it was designed in response to recommendations of Lord Laming's inquiry into the death of Victoria Climbié, specifically to allow practitioners 'to find out who else is working with the same child' (Department for Children, 2009c: 3). Lack of basic information of this type was said to be an element in the oft-reported failure of inter-agency working. A survey of practitioners in 2009 for the DCSF found that only 39 per cent of them said that the name and contact details of other professionals working with the same child were 'always' or 'usually' readily available. The ContactPoint database was significantly different from the ICS insofar as it was not designed to hold any case information (such as case notes, medical records or exam results). Instead, it holds the following information:

- Name, address, gender, date of birth and an identifying number for all children in England (up to their 18th birthday)
- Name and contact details for:

  i   Parents or carers
  ii   Educational setting (e.g., school)
  iii Primary medical practitioner (e.g., GP practice)
  iv   Other services, for example, health visitor, social worker or lead professional, and an indicator for whether a Common Assessment Framework (CAF) exists. (Department for Children, 2009c: 8)

ContactPoint may not hold detailed case information, but it is open to many thousands of professionals from many different agencies. This means that concerns about it have focused not so much on the effects on recording practice, but on the implications for civil liberties.

ContactPoint and civil liberties

Despite Baroness Morgan's claim that ContactPoint is a response to Lord Laming's recommendations (Department for Children, 2009c: 3), commentators have pointed out that government plans for such an information, referral and tracking (IRT) scheme started before the publication of Lord Laming's report (Garrett, 2009). This is significant because such plans can be linked to the government's wider agenda for e-government. Penna (2005) argues that ContactPoint is but one example of the piecemeal introduction of IRT systems that are one way of bypassing objections to a national, individual identification system. Once all children are on a database, with an ID number, then a national ID card is only another step along an accepted route. In the process, concerns about children's welfare become harder to distinguish from the practice of social surveillance and control. This is not to argue that the government is unconcerned about children's welfare or that the official aims of ContactPoint are a sham, but it is to raise awareness of the wider political context.

In fact, significant concerns about ContactPoint were raised in the House of Lords during the passage of the Children Act 2004. One aspect of the original proposals was seen as particularly problematic: the idea that practitioners should be able to put a 'flag' on the database to indicate that they had 'concerns' about a particular child. Opponents objected to the lack of clarity about when it might be appropriate to flag a concern, and whether children or their parents would be told about the flag. The result was that the government amended the legislation by removing reference to 'flags of concern'. These were replaced by an indicator that a CAF or an eCAF has been completed. Clearly, there is a possibility that the existence of such an assessment may come to be seen as a proxy for the existence of 'concerns'.

This possibility leads to concerns about the impact on families of flagging the existence of a CAF. A CAF assessment is the gateway to family support services. Even where families are actively seeking support, the knowledge that information about the CAF will be shared with other professionals who are not involved in providing the desired service may be enough to deter families from seeking such an assessment. The question here is how ContactPoint changes practice in relation to obtaining service users' consent to information sharing. Whereas the default legal position is that such consent must be obtained before information can be obtained, as the pressure group Action on Rights for Children (2010) has pointed out, the effect of ContactPoint is to remove any need for consent in order to 'populate' the database. For example, primary care trusts were the obvious place to start building a ContactPoint database because they are the only agency to hold information about all children. Primary care trusts received legal advice that they were able to provide data without parental consent, and they have done so (Carvel, 2004).

Finally, there is grave concern about the security of the ContactPoint database. It is well known that the security of a database decreases in proportion to the number of people having authorised access to it. The government's stated aims of allowing professionals to find out easily who else is working with a child implies that all professionals working with children will require access. This is a huge number of people. It is argued that some of these will be careless; others may be open to bribery; and paedophiles are likely to infiltrate the system, leading to the claim that 'it could become a search engine for paedophiles' (Carvel, 2004). Supporters respond by claiming that the data stored is very basic, such that concerns about the *consequences* (as opposed to the *likelihood*) of data loss are overstated. However, even 'basic' data such as phone number and date of birth is sensitive and has value and, as we have seen, information is also being stored that is, at the very least, indicative of 'concerns'.

ContactPoint and social work

So how should social workers have responded to the advent of ContactPoint? The first thing to recognise is the strength of what Penna (2005) describes as the 'common sense' case for ContactPoint: that it would allow professionals to know who else is working with a child. This seems a laudable and uncontroversial aim. But, by presenting ContactPoint in this way, wider questions about civil liberties and human rights may be obscured. And since social work is concerned with such questions, it falls to us to be alert to these issues.

A report for the magazine *Children and Young People Now* included the following case example.

> Staff nurse Anita Croft recently used ContactPoint when a teenage girl came into the A&E department at Royal Bolton Hospital. The girl was brought in by a paramedic, after she had been found intoxicated, wandering around town with friends. 'She only gave us her name and date of birth but from that we could let her parents know that she had been admitted and also inform her school nurse,' recalls Croft. She also passed details of the admission on to the girl's social worker for further action – and it turned out this wasn't the first time something like this had happened. (Rowntree, 2009)

This story is presented as an unproblematic example of the benefits of ContactPoint. Yet the impression given is that the young person had no say in the matter. Why did she only give her name and date of birth? Presumably she didn't want her parents, her school or her social worker to know that she was at the hospital – and she was unaware of the power of ContactPoint. What happened to her right to control her personal information? The Gillick case established the principle that a young person can consent to treatment without parental knowledge, provided that she is 'capable of making a reasonable assessment of the advantages and disadvantages of the treatment proposed' (*Gillick v. West Norfolk & Wisbech Area Health Authority* [1985] UKHL 7). Granted, there is probably insufficient information in the example for us to tell whether overriding the young person's wishes in this particular case was justified or not. But there is a serious danger that the prioritisation of information sharing, and the existence of powerful new technologies for doing so, will lead to such action being taken automatically, and not as a result of a considered professional judgement.

Conclusion

These three examples, CAF, ICS and ContactPoint, provide some pointers towards what might be considered to be good practice in the use of ICT by agencies. First, we need to recognise that professionals continue to make sense of their work by constructing narratives, and that many will find ways of importing those narratives into electronic recording systems, no matter what the system asks for. Indeed, this is a welcome development that ICT systems should be flexible enough to allow. In our view the construction of such narratives is not necessarily in opposition to the kind of identification of needs, aims and action plans that are required, for example, by the eCAF. Second, electronic systems should not be seen as a substitute for, or get in the way of, face-to-face work with service users. This has certainly been a major complaint about the ICS. Third, they should have rules about data sharing that are clear and acceptable to those whose data is being recorded and to those professionals using the system. Finally, the existence of powerful databases that enable sharing of information should not lead us to assume that information should always be shared. As we have seen in relation to ContactPoint, decisions about information sharing should be taken in the light of the rights, wishes and interests of the children and young people involved.

Taking it further

Exercise: Discussion group

We are aware that our assessment of the three examples has been critical.

Reread Chapter 1 and discuss for ONE of the examples in this chapter how it might be made fit for purpose. You will also need to follow up further reading about the example you choose, *before* you embark on the exercise.

The reason you are asked to reread the opening chapter is that you should approach this task with best practice and practice-led standards in mind. To help you avoid a merely negative stance towards ICT in agencies, you should not skate over this exercise.

6

Social Work Programmes in the Virtual World

In Chapters 3 to 5 we have travelled through the world of practice – service users, practitioners and agency context. How should the learning experience provide a jumping off point for future work for and with service users in social work agencies? We take up this question in the final two chapters of the book.

Each arriving cohort of students – social work no less than most others – has an increasing ease and familiarity with information and communication technologies. Yet it is possible that for some students – and probably for social work programme staff – this ease does not translate into optimum application to social work or use of the web, and that search strategies used are fairly basic. We said at the beginning of the book that what is entailed in a practice-led approach will be slightly different when we consider social work programmes and practice placements. The aim of this chapter is to describe, review, assess and project into the short and medium term future ways in which social work programmes – both students and academic staff – can facilitate the development of skills of evaluation, critical analysis and reflection, ability to synthesise knowledge, and problem solving; and do so in ways that promote communication, collaboration, equality of access and inclusion. A practice-led learning experience also will seek to use the communication and collaboration opportunities and possibilities offered by ICTs to creatively and flexibly embed user/carer involvement.

We talk later in the chapter about a trend towards the blurring of the conventional boundaries between what counts as practice-based learning and university-based learning. Future books on this theme may well reflect this blurring in the way they are written. But for our present purposes we keep that distinction, and focus in this chapter on the role and learning opportunities associated directly with educational institutions, and in the following chapter on the challenges and forms of practice within social work agencies and placements. Once again we aspire to take social work questions as our reference point, rather than setting out an array of skills in the form of technological competencies to acquire. We start the chapter with a brief recognition of the ways in which desired educational outcomes in this field have been expressed. We then sketch different ways that ICT developments can support learning – through hugely enhanced capacities for information searching and associated growth of resources, a sea change in how the web can offer opportunities for interactivity, the development of e-learning, and the consequences and opportunities through the increasing digitisation of material previously available only in hard copy. We reflect briefly on significant underlying trends and also on recurring concerns about the potential of these developments for good and ill. Finally, we risk peering into the future, and hazard a few guesses as to how the learning scene for aspiring social workers will change during the next decade.

Are there Requirements Social Work Students Should Meet?

When the social work degree was introduced in England in 2002, it was decided that the best way of social workers achieving IT skills was to require completion of the European Computer Driving Licence (ECDL) or equivalent. But in 2009 the General Social Care Council withdrew this requirement, whilst continuing to require that students meet the Quality Assurance Agency social work benchmark statement in respect of ICT. The details are laid out in a letter to Higher Education Institutions that is available online (Ixer, 2009).

Rafferty and Waldman have been sceptical about the ways in which the skills and knowledge needed to access and use ICT are set out in the key documents for social work training in the UK. As they express the problem,

> The skills and knowledge align more to information development and retrieval, information sharing, monitoring, recording and accessing the information base than they do to using information and communication technology as a practice method for engaging directly with service users. (Rafferty and Waldman, 2006: 13)

It is certainly the case that the UK requirement for part of the first decade of the century, that social work students should be assessed as competent to the level of the European Computer Driving Licence, while it had some value as setting minimum levels, reflected 'the basic building blocks of IT literacy skills rather than any wider vision of how information and communication technologies can be used across social work learning and practice' (Rafferty and Waldman, 2006: 14).

In the broad sense outlined in the opening paragraph of the chapter it is helpful to use the expression e-learning, or perhaps more cumbersomely 'technology enhanced learning', to refer to the increasing diversity of technological developments and approaches. Yet definitions of e-learning range from quite narrow to very broad. This is partly because the way e-learning has come to be understood is developing year by year. One commentator has argued that a weakness in initial ways of seeing e-learning was that it did not fit with the aim of supporting professional competence development. Rather, it facilitated the straightforward transfer of knowledge (Ehlers, 2007). In harmony with the approach we have taken in this book, Ehlers concludes that

> The focus in the discussion about how e-learning can make a difference, moved from e-learning as a *technological innovation* to e-learning as a *pedagogical innovation* and today has arrived at a discussion about the strategic level – how e-learning can make a difference through stimulating a new learning and organisational culture. (Ehlers, 2007: 188)

Knowledge transfer will not, in itself, enable users to gain professional competence. One way of describing this development is to see it as a change from e-learning as a way of distributing information and knowledge, to a form of collaborative learning. We should not overstate this, or throw out all initiatives from more than a few years back, as early e-learning packages usually included exercise work and elements of interactivity, though nowhere near the subsequent level of developments. The development of welfare benefit packages was another early player in this field.[1]

The Practice of Technology as a Social Work Student

We sketched in Chapter 2 the range of ICT developments that have shaped social work, and it is probably true that this has nowhere been more apparent than within social work programmes and in universities. They have changed – and will continue to change – the range, volume and capacity for searching digital resources, the continued expansion and diversification of e-learning, the possibilities for interactive learning, and the remarkable possibilities for access to newly digitised archives.

---

[1] See http://www.ferret.co.uk/main/index.asp?menu=5.42&page=1 for a continuing commercial example.

Learning resources

The volume and range of digital learning resources available to university students has increased almost exponentially during the last few years. Students commencing their study three or four years before the time of writing would have expected, for example, to find journals primarily available as hard copies on library shelves, and that library holdings would represent only a fraction of journals in any given field. Within the space of a single undergraduate time span this has changed such that the primary mode of journal use is through access to extensive sources accumulated by bulk purchases of bundles of hundreds of electronic journals at a time, so that once someone has carried out a search of publications of a topic of their interest, it is likely that 70 or 80 per cent of those will be available in full copy format.

A growth in the ease and power of search capacity has emerged alongside these resources. This has quickly led to increasing expectations that student assignments – essays, projects and dissertations – should display a familiarity with and demonstrable use of these resources.

For social work students – primarily in the UK but of course beyond – an important and invaluable add-on to these developments has been the advent of the Social Care Institute for Excellence (SCIE). In addition to commissioning e-learning resources for the health and social care sector, SCIE thus far has been able to make its whole range of publications available online and free to all users.[2] It is a major resource that has limited echoes in other countries. Alongside this development should be included the presence of a social work and social policy subject centre, one of 24 such centres, set up to enhance the student learning experience by promoting high quality learning, teaching and assessment (http://www.swap.ac.uk/). As an adjunct to the provision of resources, SCIE has developed extended guidance on the mechanics of undertaking more systematic ways of reviewing social work and social care research (Coren and Fisher, 2006).

Scoping studies are imprecisely defined but usually consist of one or more discrete components; most commonly they are non-systematic reviews of the literature, but other important elements are literature mapping, conceptual mapping and policy mapping. Some scoping studies also involve consultations with stakeholders including the end users of research. Scoping studies have been used for a wide variety of purposes, although a common feature is to identify questions and topics for future research. (Anderson et al., 2008)

---

[2]There is a corresponding body in Scotland, the Institute for Research and Innovation in the Social Services (IRISS) http://www.iriss.org.uk/.

We would demur from this otherwise helpful statement at one point. Scoping studies, as they are best understood and used, are certainly undertaken in a more systematic, planned and transparent way than the traditional narrative reviews of literature that hitherto characterised most social work course assignments.

An example of a student scoping study may help. This student, consistent with the Anderson definition above, was combining a scoping study of research on social work's engagement with the education of traveller children with plans for two key informant interviews. Table 6.1 records her

TABLE 6.1   *Scoping study: Education, social work and traveller children*[T1]

Date		Database searched	Keywords used	Hits	Relevant hits	After removing duplicated hits	Used after full reading
10/11	1	e-prints soton (University of Southampton) Search for Key Informant Interview publications	Traveller AND Education	23	10	3	2
9/01	1	Informa-World (through Metalib gateway)	Traveller Education	17	6	1	2
9/01	1	ASSIA	Traveller	21	10	3	2
	2	ESSCO	Education	20	8	2	2
	3	ISI	AND	3	0	0	0
	4	PsycInfo	Social Policy	14	2	2	1
	5	Social Care Online	AND Social Work	18	5	3	1
	6	Social Services Abstracts		14	2	0	1
11/03	1	CSA Illuminata (through ASSIA)	Travellers AND Education AND Social Work	55	14	3	4
31/03	1	ASSIA	Social Work AND	2	1	0	1
	2	ISI	Settled Traveller	1	1	1	0
	3	PsycInfo	AND	2	1	1	0
	4	CSA Illuminata	Social Services	14	6	5	1
	5	ZETOC		2	2	2	0
Totals	10	databases used (UK and non UK)		206	68	26	17

'Hits': Number of journal articles identified on individual databases within the search criteria.
'Relevant': Journal articles identified through reading the abstracts as potentially relevant to the scoping study.
'Duplicated': Journal articles excluded because replicated within that search or other previously conducted searches
'Used': Journal articles that are discovered in that search and are not duplicated from previous searches, and are included in final scoping study.[T2]

[T1] This is used with slightly edited notes with permission of Becki Scotter who completed a social work degree in 2009.
[T2] A variation on scoping studies is a review strategy often referred to as *systematic mapping* (Clapton et al., 2009).

search terms, when she undertook the searches and her results step by step from initial 'hits' through to the eventual inclusion of research studies.

e-Learning

We referred to Ehlers' observation of how there has been a change from e-learning as a way of distributing information and knowledge, to a form of collaborative learning. It is helpful in this connection to reproduce in full Rafferty and Waldman's elaboration of the various dimensions of e-learning, which reflects this development but retains aspects of the earlier way of understanding e-learning. It provides a helpful template for students – and academic staff – to plan and monitor their learning and teaching.

1   Formal knowledge and learning resources

    a   A method of learning pre-developed curriculum content;
    b   A means of 'packaging' various learning resources to tailor learning to the student;
    c   Access to knowledge and information through databases of research evidence, abstracts, full text journals, web based information, legislation, law and practice.

2   Learning networks

    a   A means of learning collaboratively: student to student, group to group, student to educator and educator to student;
    b   An ability to learn across and within: courses, organisations and multi and inter-professionally.

3   Contact, administration and assessment

    a   A mode of formative and summative assessment;
    b   A means of supporting the administration and tracking of learning.

4   Information management skills

    a   Ensuring the baseline skills of students and staff include appropriate levels of IT skills to support learning and practice;
    b   Development of information literacy, including the critical appraisal skills necessary to make use of online resources;
    c   As a subject in its own right in terms of learning about the effective and ethical use of IT within social care (Rafferty and Waldman, 2006: 17).

Two examples of rather different approaches to e-learning resources are represented by the work of SCIE and IRISS. SCIE has developed a series of e-learning resources that look at principles of good communication skills in a range of contexts. These can be downloaded to virtual learning environments in universities (http://www.scie.org.uk/publications/elearning/index.asp). IRISS has a useful and much under-appreciated range of podcasts on a mix of topics (well over 100 at the time of writing), several of which are associated with reports from work that IRISS has commissioned (http://www.iriss.org.uk/rss/podcast/sieswe.xml). There may be future career opportunities for social workers with an interest in this field, stemming from the gradual movement to professionalise e-learning seen, for example, in opportunities to seek professional accreditation for e-learning responsibilities, as well as getting involved in professional networks of e-learning practitioners (Donovan and Saxon, 2009).[3]

Web 2.0 and interactive learning

One of us recalls the impact – delighted amazement in one or two cases – when students in a social work class in the mid 1990s sent emails to pre-arranged cooperative academic colleagues in other countries, and received immediate replies. He also recalls annually tracking the number of email users in the world, as it rose from six to seven figures. The speed and scale of development is easy to miss. But it was perhaps the immediacy of the interaction across oceans and time zones that so enticed those students.

Much of the focus in recent learning developments has been captured in discussion of what is usually referred to as Web 2.0. We noted in Chapter 2 that the term 'Web 2.0' reflects a shift away from 'static' web pages towards web applications that allow people to collaborate and share information online. Examples include social networking sites, video sharing sites, wikis and blogs. But the term is often used in a looser sense to refer to a broader shift towards interactive and collaborative e-learning – echoing once more Ehlers' remark about distributive and collaborative learning. An excellent commentary on this development has been edited by Selwyn (2008) which, though aimed initially at those who develop and deliver the learning experience, is helpful as a student resource to understand the debates and issues that this development brings to the fore. Though using terms that for some readers will call for a quick googling, Selwyn summarises Web 2.0 as follows:

> 'Web 2.0' is an umbrella term for a host of recent internet applications such as social networking, wikis, folksonomies, virtual societies, blogging, multiplayer online gaming and 'mash-ups'. Whilst differing in form and function, all these applications share a common characteristic of supporting internet-based interaction between and within groups. (Selwyn, 2008: 4)

---

[3]See the Association of Learning Technology professional accreditation process for e-learning practitioners at http://www.alt.ac.uk/.

It thus makes a break from forms of learning that have marked most university and schooling, in that, in addition to being interactive, 'information is shared "many-to-many" rather than being transmitted "one-to-many"' (Selwyn, 2008: 4). The best-known example that perhaps illustrates this is Wikipedia, which is an open document, created, updated and refereed by its readers, thus deriving its authority from ongoing group discussion and consensus rather than the word of a single expert, as in, for example, the *Encyclopaedia Britannica*.

Crook (in Selwyn, 2008: 9) helpfully identifies the learning concepts that lie behind Web 2.0. He sees them as fourfold:

1   Collaboration between learners.
2   Publication, in the sense that we expect to see the work of learners on display. This is often expressed in the phrase 'read-and-write' to describe the dual role of the user.
3   New forms of literacy are present that go beyond the printed word.
4   Web 2.0 offers new ways for learners to conduct personal research. In doing so it poses problems of authority and the ephemeral nature of web 'knowledge'.

He also suggests that Web 2.0 typically realises four human dispositions by socialising the playful, the expressive, the reflective and the exploratory. How should we – both students and programme staff – respond to these developments? Should we embrace them wholesale or observe a more circumspect stance? Selwyn observes that growing numbers of commentators are urging teachers and education institutions to maintain an air of interested but uninvolved detachment, recognising Web 2.0 as a space for learners and informal learning rather than for teachers and the formal provision of learning (Selwyn, 2008: 24). Like them, we do not believe this will prove either feasible or desirable.

One of the most common ways in which Web 2.0 begins to creep into social work programmes is through developments in local virtual learning environments (VLEs). VLEs initially developed as a means of depositing lectures, often through PowerPoint slides, for distributing information about assignments, and for making announcements. Step by step these are now incorporating interactive dimensions. For example, module-linked discussion boards through which students can pose questions to staff and fellow students, or respond to such questions, are becoming routine elements in most social work programmes (e.g., Cooner, 2010).

New learning forms of this kind raise new questions about learning community netiquette.

Exercise 6.1   Learning community netiquette

Devise a list of netiquette guidance that you think would help for posting and responding to messages on a discussion board.

After spending perhaps ten minutes on this, compare your list with one we have included at the end of the chapter on p. 109.

It is a commonplace observation that university staff who teach computing science know less than most of their students about the latest developments and skills of ICT. In a corresponding way, those who teach on social work programmes find it difficult to keep up with developments. Repositories of learning exist, such as the hugely successful website set up by Russell Stannard at the University of Westminster, which acts as a repository for training videos. It is geared towards both students and teachers. For example, there are free videos on using iTunes, Twitter, Wikis, Second Life, podcasting, Notice Board and many others (http://www.russellstannard.com/). The initiative gained an award as the outstanding ICT initiative for 2008[4] for its innovation and impact and also because of its commitment to open access.

Archives

It may be assumed that the growth of digital resources is a development that only benefits newly published resources. That is fortunately not the case. The process of digitally scanning and storing previous hard copy archives is rapidly making available opportunities to access those deposits. Social work has a short history, but one that is too easily neglected. It is as if we are 'too embarrassed to look seriously at our history, afraid of the disorder we might find, too eager to distance ourselves from the pre-professional beginnings' and are, in consequence, homeless and 'disembedded' (Lorenz, 2007: 599). Lorenz concludes that 'All social work practices are deeply embedded in historical and cultural habits from which we cannot detach ourselves at will'. He aptly infers from this that we should be practising history 'in the dual sense of positioning ourselves in a historical context and of giving our interventions a historical dimension' (Lorenz, 2007: 610). To express it more simply, knowledge about the past is helpful in shaping the future. Knowing about the work and life of Arnold Toynbee,

---

[4]By JISC (the Joint Information Systems Committee) and the *Times Higher Education* magazine

Jane Addams, Mary Richmond, Ann Hartman and many other social work pioneers is not only a matter of curiosity. Many of social work's current challenges are not that different from those in the past. Some years ago the concern about a lack of knowledge about general history in the Netherlands resulted in the highly popular format of a 'history canon', which was quickly adopted for social work, both in the Netherlands and in Flanders. The positive feedback on both projects, as well as international interest in the format, provided the background for the subsequent development of a history of social work initiative at www.historyofsocialwork.org.

   This is an area where progressively available archives will help. Take, for example, social work journals. The early years of social work were associated with several influential journals, some of which are available through JSTOR, and the number available will continue to grow year on year. This immediately opens up and provides evidence to test and challenge accepted preconceptions about how social work courses developed 80 or 90 years ago. JSTOR, so its home page advises,

> is a not-for-profit service that helps scholars, researchers, and students discover, use, and build upon a wide range of content in a trusted digital archive of over one thousand academic journals and other scholarly content. We use information technology and tools to increase productivity and facilitate new forms of scholarship. (JSTOR, 2010)

Then what about newspaper archives? A digital archive such as Nexis UK http://www.lexisnexis.org.uk/nexis/ readily enables anything from a search of all papers over a long period to searches of a given paper for a short period. By way of illustration, we undertook a brief search of the *New York Times* for the 12-month period prior to our search. It revealed that 'social work' appeared in the paper on 130 occasions. Nexis UK displays the full text with the search terms highlighted. Social work was mentioned 111 times in the London *Times* over the same period – one preoccupied with the aftermath of the case of Baby Peter, killed in the London borough of Haringey.[5] Social work students have often expressed convictions about how social work is represented in the press. Resources of this kind make research much more feasible at dissertation level. 'Students love it' was a comment on Nexis UK by the social work subject librarian in our university.

---

[5] For the same papers and the ten-year period from 2000 to 2010 there were almost twice as many 'hits' for the *New York Times* compared with the London *Times* (1,469 and 800), but impressionistically the kind of coverage was rather dissimilar.

An Aside: Trends

What general trends can we detect as already relatively firmly established in recent developments? We think there are two: first, a boundary blurring; second, a shift to new forms of learning in the virtual world.

Boundary blurring

There are two connected areas of blurring. First, as we noted earlier in the chapter, the boundaries between *practice-based* learning and *university-based* learning are step by step becoming fuzzier as a consequence of increased potential for shared access by agencies and universities to new resources. The point should not be overstated, for the boundary has never been watertight – practice teachers have always advised students on reading they have found helpful. For decades, universities have engaged in simulated forms of learning through role play, video work on skills and so forth. Also, practice teachers and agency staff are regularly invited to contribute to university-based learning and teaching. But the shift is real nonetheless. The quickest way to realise this is to scan again Chapter 4, and consider how the practice developments outlined there have potential implications for boundary blurring between agency and university, as sites of learning.

The second arena for boundary blurring is that between *formal and informal learning*. This is most clearly apparent when we think of the challenges raised by Web 2.0, communities of practice (see Chapter 4), and their likely successors. We may think of ICT as providing a means whereby we can do the things that were done before more efficiently; or as a means of enhancing what was done before; or possibly, as a means of doing something that was not done at all before (Rafferty and Waldman, 2006: 18). The less that learning is tied to the institution, the fuzzier the boundaries become between learning and location. An interesting notion in this connection is that of the 'Edgeless University' – a term that recognises how technology makes it possible for learning and research to take place in new places, often outside the university. This development is likely to affect those who teach as well as those who learn, in that programmes can increasingly be delivered from off campus.

Forms of learning

The second general trend is that affecting *how we learn in a virtual world*. Technology challenges how we think about the way we should learn. Consider the following concepts and distinctions:

- Synchronous and asynchronous learning
- Hybrid or blended learning
- Distributed, distance and online learning

The first distinction draws attention to the difference between whether or not collaborative and interactive learning takes place for participants at the same time. Video conferencing, online chat rooms, and whiteboards are synchronous, whereas discussion boards and virtual learning environments are asynchronous. One possible advantage of the latter is that it allows students to work at their own pace. However, misunderstandings may occur and are less easy to correct than in face-to-face learning (Finn, 2008). Blended learning refers to a mix of face-to-face learning and, for instance, video conferencing and online learning. The distinctions between distributed, distanced and online learning are straightforward.

These changes have consequences for how we should think about assessment of learning. For example, there are emerging e-assessment technologies to promote innovative practices such as just-in-time assessment and peer review. One way this may be developed would be the implementation of a web-based stage-by-stage formative assessment strategy, designed to enable the student to provide the lecturer with an advance indication of her readiness for an upcoming face-to-face session. Describing an application of this approach, Carrington and Green say that students were given a small set of questions in advance, intended to lead them into the topic of the next seminar or lecture. They were then:

> required to submit electronically their responses to these questions some 12 to 24 hours before the face-to-face session. The idea was that these responses would enable the lecturer to see where the students in the class were situated with respect to the topic under discussion, and to make corresponding adjustments to the forthcoming class. The face-to-face session would then be sensitive to both the needs and strengths of the students, rather than being a set piece designed by the lecturer; hence the 'Just in Time' title of the approach. (Carrington and Green, 2007)

Developments like this are likely to lead to a more interactive approach for the face-to-face sessions.

'Interactive' in this context is likely to mean two main things. First, there should be a proper integration of the results of the student pre-class activity into the face-to-face discussion; consideration of that pre-class work should not just be bolted on to the session as a preamble or postscript but should play an explicit and pivotal role in the discussion. Second, if the session is a lecture, it should include short periods designated for collaborative group learning, where small groups of students work together to solve problems.

Is All This a Good Thing?

We started this chapter by referring to the development of skills of evaluation, critical analysis and reflection, ability to synthesise knowledge, and problem solving. But these skills and qualities are no more likely to emerge automatically from the use of ICT than from attending lectures or seminars. We also mentioned that Web 2.0 offers new ways for learners to conduct personal research, but in doing so it poses problems of authority and the ephemeral nature of web 'knowledge'. This is in part because knowledge structures are 'not navigated with the same tools or the same ease as more traditional documentary collections' (Crook, 2008: 9). 'In adopting Web 2.0, education will have to confront the challenge of cultivating learner discernment as well as that of stimulating learner participation' (Crook, 2008: 7).

Educational fears about the web sometimes have been expressed. Does online learning lead to people becoming disengaged, alienated or disconnected from education? Does it undermine an essential dimension of relationship building in social work learning and teaching? Are traditional skills and literacies being neglected and withering on the vine? Are universities conniving in the creation of a Google-generation incapable of independent critical thought – a dumbing down of education? Does it lead to a realignment of power between learner and teacher?[6] Rather differently, is Web 2.0 leading to increased surveillance?

Each of these questions is best understood when it is related to student culture. For example, in a research study of student values and attitudes in the USA regarding plagiarism, Blum concludes that there is a disconnection between student attitudes towards how to cite sources, and conventions among academic staff. She develops the interesting argument that one of the reasons why students may plagiarise with apparently so few misgivings may be associated with a move to a more 'social' self which is 'performed' through the internet, cell phones and the like, leading to a trend and pressure towards a round the clock connectivity. This pressure towards collaboration is reinforced by universities with changes towards group modes of assessment. In this social context, ideas of demonstrating originality may be less socially important than maintaining social networks (Blum, 2009). In this context, our position is that we need to think how social work education can change the web as well as how the web can change social work education. We need to remain discerning about when social work or academic principles and values may hold fast, and when a

---

[6]Perhaps as in the rating site where academics are rated for helpfulness, clarity, and easiness, with an option to rate whether or not they are hot, http://www.ratemyprofessors.com/ and associated YouTube postings.

particular practice which involves a technology engenders or possibly requires a change in these.

The Future

This final part of the chapter is deliberately speculative.[7] Some developments are already present. Others, while technologically feasible, are less certain. Either way, a reader of this book in a few years' time will doubtless smile at the undue optimism and lack of vision of this future gaze. We risk disregarding the Danish physicist, Neils Bohr's wise counsel, 'Never express yourself more clearly than you are able to think'.

e-books

The 2010 Horizon report anticipates that by 2013 electronic books will be fully established as part of learning resources (New Media Consortium and EDUCAUSE Learning Initiative, 2010). The argument is a fuller one than those hearing the argument at the point it was written may realise. For e-books to be so established it will require 'convenient and capable electronic reading devices [that] combine the activities of acquiring, storing, reading, and annotating digital books, making it very easy to collect and carry hundreds of volumes in a space smaller than a single paperback book' (New Media Consortium and EDUCAUSE Learning Initiative, 2010). Such devices are already present, but when linked to the probable impact of mobile technology on pedagogy, this could have a major influence. We anticipate this development is likely to be the key driver of change at the point when this book is published. The Horizon report points to three drags on development of e-books for education:

> The primary obstacle was simply availability. While a great variety of consumer titles are available electronically, textbooks or academic works have been published in electronic formats far less frequently. Secondly, as the reader technology developed, the ability to easily render high quality illustrations was initially limited. The last obstacle was related to the publishing model. Where electronic versions were available, they were most commonly viewed as ancillary to the printed version, which had to be purchased before the electronic version could be accessed – and the early versions were not in formats compatible with most readers.

---

[7]We acknowledge our indebtedness to the 2010 Horizon Report.

These obstacles are being overcome. For example, 'The newest readers can display graphics of all kinds and make it easy to bookmark and annotate pages and passages. Annotations can be exported, viewed online, shared, and archived. In addition, electronic readers offer keyword searching, instant dictionary lookups and, in some cases, wireless Internet access' (New Media Consortium and EDUCAUSE Learning Initiative, 2010).

MyLibrary offers a good example of such developments (http://www.myilibrary.com/). It is the largest e-books platform allowing searches, creating and editing notes, and bookmarks. It has a flexible choice of how to search and will show full text hits from the search criteria used. It is still in its infancy in that, at the point of writing, there were only 26 titles that had 'social work' in the key words and only 265 with social work mentioned somewhere in the full text. A quick login and check as you read this will show if and how quickly the resource has grown.

Mobile learning and edgeless social work courses

E-books lead into a wider idea of mobile learning, by which we refer to the use of network-capable devices, such as cell phones and iPods that students are already carrying, and the ability to download learning materials. The opportunities are extensive because virtually all higher education students carry some form of mobile device, and the cellular network that supports their connectivity continues to grow. Mobile learning is starting to be established on many campuses, 'although before we see widespread use, concerns about privacy, classroom management, and access will need to be addressed' (New Media Consortium and EDUCAUSE Learning Initiative, 2010).

Open education

The likely development of open educational resources also appears to be quite major in its potential implications. 'Open' in this context refers to access to the materials. This links of course with existing facilities such as virtual learning environments, but it is the open access element that is different. The main social work engagement with this has come from OpenLearn – the UK's Open University initiative (http://www.open.ac.uk/openlearn/home.php?gclid=CMfaqeT2pqECFYts4wodJ2zdFw). The site holds quite a lot of social work learning material. There are very big initiatives that involve both high flying universities – Massachusetts Institute of Technology (MIT) has gone for this in a very major way – and less well known universities. The 2010 Horizon report is again upbeat:

Part of the appeal of open content is that it is also a response to both the rising costs of traditionally published resources and the lack of educational resources in some regions, and a cost-effective alternative to textbooks and other materials. As customizable educational content is made increasingly available for free over the Internet, students are learning not only the material, but also skills related to finding, evaluating, interpreting, and repurposing the resources they are studying in partnership with their teachers.

iTunes U is a further development in this context (http://www.apple.com/education/itunes-u/). It has interest for social work, as at the time of writing over 600 universities are using it, including influential universities like Oxford, and about half of them are providing it as open access. Hence we can foresee a further blurring of boundaries to add to those we discussed earlier – in this case boundaries between one social work programme and another as students begin to use material from open resources. There are two ways that social work students may use such material. First, it may help as 'pre-course' experience to try out their interest in social work. Second, those already on courses may use it to supplement their learning experience. OpenLearn (http://openlearn.open.ac.uk/) (a freely downloadable online resource from The Open University in the UK) has also worked with a Children's Services Department to provide a workforce development unit for existing staff.

Barely a month goes by without a further initiative of this general kind. Mendeley – 'like iTunes for research papers' as it describes itself – is a free research management tool (www.mendeley.com/). But it operates as more than a database from which papers can be downloaded. It has capacity for users to upload papers, and it is extensively interactive. It is early to foresee how such initiatives may develop. Developments of this kind will need a critical mass. In its early manifestation it is aimed at research teams rather than students, and there are very few recognisably social work papers on the site. It is still at beta testing stage, and is not obviously simple to use. But the potential for social work applications, especially if associated with informal learning sites, is very considerable.

Social work in developing countries

These initiatives – in principle at least – have implications for social work education in developing countries. We referred above to the 2010 Horizon Report's remarks about open learning and content that *'part of the appeal of open content is that it is also a response to both the rising costs of traditionally published resources and the lack of educational resources in some regions, and a cost-effective alternative to textbooks and other materials'* (italics added).

A world summit on the information society was held in Switzerland (2003) and Tunisia (2005) and it included, among other statements, a Declaration of Principles, in which it was acknowledged:

> We are ... fully aware that the benefits of the information technology revolution are today unevenly distributed between the developed and developing countries and within societies. We are fully committed to turning this digital divide into a digital opportunity for all, particularly for those who risk being left behind and being further marginalized. (http://www.itu.int/wsis/docs/geneva/official/dop.html)

The general concerns about the 'digital divide' have special resonance in this context. But to our knowledge the work required to make this happen has not been done (Rye and Zubaidah, 2008). While many students in developing countries – the majority world – use English language texts, or those texts translated into their own languages, there remains a major task of applying and 'translating' to local cultures and service patterns. Indeed there are some intra-UK policy transfer issues even within the exercises we have suggested at the close of this chapter. Website development for social work programmes in developing countries is still patchy and in some cases very rudimentary. However, this does seem an area where mutual interest would repay collaborative efforts.

Virtual worlds

We mentioned earlier the website associated with Russell Stannard at the University of Westminster. One initiative that he was pursuing at the turn of the first decade was to set up videos to support the development of Virtual Worlds (http://www.theconsultants-e.com/).

> The term virtual world refers to a computer-based environment, and encompasses online games such as World of Warcraft as well as social worlds such as Second Life. Virtual worlds play host to collaboration, creative production and dissemination, socialising, role-play, programming and building. (Carr, 2008: 13)

Carr's article helpfully introduces the reader to educational applications of virtual worlds, in particular the best known example, Second Life (http://secondlife.com/?v=1.1). An interesting example of partial adoption of ideas of virtual worlds is provided in a valuable article on creating a cross-cultural virtual learning environment for social work students to explore racism, past and present, in the UK, South Africa and the USA

(Buchanan et al., 2008). The issues were addressed through a four-week online conference. Three sets of 'conference papers' were prepared by one of the authors as a basis for a series of asynchronous discussions. Poetry, YouTube clips, discussion board debates, video lectures, and online questionnaires were used. The three discussion boards yielded 174, 168 and 178 contributions respectively. While this was quite a long way from a fully developed virtual world it produced a fascinating learning experience.

A more ambitious example is the Inter-Life Project led by Victor Lally, and supported by UK research council funding. As at 2010 the Inter-Life Project had successfully created two virtual island environments in consultation with users/participants:

- InterLife Island 1 for 18+ young people to work on school-to-university and within-university transitions;
- InterLife Island 2 where pre-18s (14–17) could work on transitions related to their 'dually-exceptional' status.

The project had also achieved a flexible working integration of mobile devices with the islands, and created sophisticated in-world data gathering for the analysis of interactions. In parallel, the project team had developed an open source InterLife Island using the Open Sim environment. All of this has been complemented by the negotiation and nurturing of educational partnerships with user groups in regional education authorities and schools. One aim of this was to share the potential of the island environments and begin to develop functioning learning communities with these partners, engaging in a wide range of in-world activities. The obvious analogies with issues relevant to social work service users suggest ways in which this may transfer and develop.[8]

A more tentative associated strand of development is *augmented reality*, i.e., 'The concept of blending (augmenting) virtual data – information, rich media, and even live action – with what we see in the real world, for the purpose of enhancing the information we can perceive with our senses' (New Media Consortium and EDUCAUSE Learning Initiative, 2010). There are already possible applications in medicine, and applications in the social care field may involve home-based technologies for care and illness management. Such developments are again likely to be driven by the development of mobile technology.

---

[8]Based on personal communication from Victor Lally, April 2010.

So much for social work programme futures. We open the final chapter with a scenario that provokes reflection on how such developments may shape practice learning in the future.

Taking it further

Ehlers' article on e-learning (2007) is an interesting academic but fairly accessible discussion of what we mean by the various main concepts linked to e-learning and competence, and is worth following up by readers who wish to take their thinking further.

We have intentionally cited several other sources that would not be included in most social work reading lists. These are also offered as a resource for taking your understanding and interest further.

Answers to Exercise 6.1 Community netiquette

A possible rule set for such discussion boards (Exercise 6.1, p. 99) might include the following:

- Check whether you wish to add a post to an existing thread or start a new thread.
- Always use a clear message header.
- Always sign your messages.
- Aim for correct spelling and punctuation.
- Have a 'reader focus' and keep posts succinct.
- Be positive: acknowledge and support your fellow students.
- Avoid sarcasm, irony or shouting (writing in CAPITALS).
- Use emoticons to clarify your meaning.
- If you want to disagree with someone, start by restating what you think they have said in your own words.
- Consider how you will deal with information that may involve considerations of confidentiality.
- Briefly state the relevance of any links to external websites you include.

Consider how you might extend this list to accommodate engagement with Web 2.0 tools. For example, how would you maintain boundaries between your professional and private identity?

(Continued)

(Continued)

Exercise 6.2 Group exercise

Access the store of podcasts on the IRISS site at: http://www.iriss.
org.uk/rss/podcast/sieswe.xml.
  Either

(a) Choose and agree two or three linked podcasts that fall in your
     group's area of interest. Arrange for a discussion board to be set
     up for a limited period for group members to post comments
     and responses.

Or

(b) As part of a seminar or discussion board exercise, each member
     listens in advance to one podcast agreed in advance. If it is still
     there, this could be the podcast on *Web 2.0 and Informal Learning*:
     http://www.iriss.org.uk/node/245.

7

ICT and Practice Based Learning

The mainstream[1] view of social work education regards the practice placement as an integral part of learning, and of critical importance in the learning process. The argument is that whilst on placement, students gain the opportunity to integrate theory, practice and research in a supervised environment. And it is this integration that many see as 'the essence of social work both as a profession and as a field of study' (Sherraden and Sherraden, 2000: 61). This chapter considers the relationship between ICT and the process of practice learning. We saw in the previous chapter how Virtual Learning Environments (VLEs) have become a regular part of teaching and learning in universities across the UK. In this chapter we will consider how they might relate to practice learning. But we should note that ICT has the potential to support practice learning in ways that go beyond the current capabilities of university VLEs. Consider the following scenario. We have taken into account that there will be limits on access to file downloads and other resources via agencies.

Example 7.1

Paul is a social work student on a university qualifying social work programme in England. Paul is on placement with a social work agency near where he lives but, because of the local demography, opportunities for working with diverse

(Continued)

---

[1]One dissenting voice has called recently for initial academic training in England to be separated from subsequent practice training, following the model used in the legal profession (Lombard, 2010).

(Continued)

communities are limited. Today, he is about to take part in a virtual role play, using 3D video technology, with Kam, an Asian service user who is in an office several hundred miles away. Kam is a member of a mental health service user organisation that is working closely with the university to contribute to research and to social work training. Also present in the 'virtual' room will be Narinder, Paul's practice teacher and Jenny, his onsite mentor. Other students who are members of Paul's learning group are able to watch from computers across the internet. All participants are wearing 3D glasses connected to lightweight and portable, internet-connected hand-held computers with built-in web cams. The role play lasts about an hour and is followed by an extensive debriefing. Paul comments on how the 3D video link added the kind of fluidity and access to emotion that made it begin to feel like it was real practice.

This 3D scenario may seem unlikely even today, but in fact it was suggested as long ago as 2004 that this kind of thing might be happening in 2010. The specific scenario described above was originally envisaged in a speculative article by Cooner (2004; cf. Rockinson-Szapkiw and Walker, 2009). Cooner argued that anticipated developments in ICT offered significant opportunities for innovative developments in practice learning – not least because of the ability of ICT to overcome barriers of space and time – but that new developments should support the principles and ethos of social work.

Cooner's approach might well be considered an example of what we have called 'technology-led', insofar as it starts by considering anticipated technologies and then imagining suitable social work applications, in this case in practice learning. In this chapter we will consider ICT in the context of practice learning but, in line with our preferred approach, we will start with the business of practice learning itself. Our account of practice learning is seen from the perspective of students in training. So the chapter begins with the processes of finding and setting up your placement, before moving on to consider the experience of learning on placement, and the process of evaluating it. However, it should be made clear that the process of learning in and through practice does not stop at the point of qualification. Because of this the chapter extends to include continuing professional development and ICT.

Finding and Setting Up Your Placement

Whereas universities used to maintain paper lists of agencies that might provide social work placements, along with names of practice teachers and workplace supervisors, the trend is for these to be held electronically, often on databases. As we saw in Chapter 6, Rafferty and Waldman have provided a helpful way of thinking about developments in e-learning. They further suggest that:

> Creative and skilled use of e-learning resources can shift the model of social work education from:
>
>> Stage 1 – Replacement (using online technology to do the same task as before); and
>> Stage 2 – Enhancement (using online technology to enhance what you did before) to:
>> Stage 3 – Transformation (using online technology to do what you couldn't do before). (2003: iii)

In these terms, moving paper records of placement providers on to an IT system is an example of a 'replacement' activity. However, by doing so it is possible to create opportunities for 'enhancement' and 'transformation'. For example, in the UK, staff at Bournemouth have used the university VLE to develop a facility known as 'Placements Online'. This contains:

> 'replacement' activity, e.g. the posting of news, information, assignment guidelines and course documents …

and:

> 'enhancement' activity, e.g. hyperlinks to web based resources and to maps to locate the placement agency and agency websites including individualised access to placement allocation/practice teacher details. (Quinney, 2005: 441)

Students have reported positively on the way in which these enhanced features make placement matching both quicker and more straightforward. We will return to the 'transformative' aspects of 'Placements Online' in the next section.

In addition to developments at individual universities, there is in England a national programme to implement a web-based information system to support the professional development of social workers at pre- and post-qualifying levels. The system is known as LeaRNS: it is being developed by Skills for Care and funded by the Department of Health (Skills for Care, 2010c). The system is very ambitious in scope, and we will explore some of its wider functions later in the chapter. For the moment we should note that one of its central functions is to provide:

up-to-date and easily accessible information about the availability of placements, and people who can supervise and assess students. (Skills for Care, 2009)

The idea is that employers will update the relevant information about placements that may be on offer, along with details of supervisors, and make them available to the universities with whom they work. Employers will be able to 'broadcast' the availability of placements if they so desire, but Skills for Care stress that this is a confidential and secure system where each organisation retains control over its own data. Sharing of data only takes place with the explicit agreement of the agency – technically via a simple 'handshake' arrangement. Members of university staff are then able to use the system to streamline the process of 'matching' students to placements. A report on the pilot at Birmingham City University suggests that students can also access the system to complete placement application forms and to see details of offered placements (Skills for Care, 2010a).

The LeaRNS system was piloted at eight universities between 2007 and 2009, but at the time of writing evaluations had not yet been published. Nonetheless, at this stage it seems that this will be a significant development, having received the backing of the General Social Care Council (GSCC)[2] and the Association of Directors of Adult Social Services (ADASS).

Support for Learning on Placement

Much university-based learning in social work takes place in the context of small groups. Typically, in the early stages of their training, students get to know a consistent group of their peers, with whom they interact and learn, both formally and informally. The first placement may then represent a sharp break with this pattern. Students on placement are often physically distant from the university, they may be the only student placed at the practice agency, and there is a significant risk that they will feel isolated from their student peer group. They must rapidly develop a more independent style of learning.

Group learning

Partly in order to counter some of the difficulties that students may experience when starting their first placement, universities are beginning to develop online support groups for students on placement. In this section

---

[2]The UK government announced in July 2010 the planned abolition of the General Social Care Council.

we will examine two such models that have been reported in the literature: one in England and one in the US.

First, the 'Placements Online' system at the University of Bournemouth in England (Quinney, 2005) does more than hold information about placements in order to help with matching and setting up of placements. It also supports 'transformative' activity, in the form of a discussion forum that allows asynchronous communication (not in real time) between students, with a member of academic staff acting as a moderator. Initial topics for discussion were set by the moderator, based partly on student views expressed at a (face-to-face) pre-placement focus group meeting. As the placement progressed, students began to take more ownership of the discussion topics.

The use of the discussion forum was monitored and formally evaluated, and the main findings were as follows. First, there had been some concern that students might not use the facility. In fact, of the cohort of 28 students, 22 used the forum at some stage and 13 were regular contributors. Given that use of the forum was voluntary and not contributing to assessment, this is reported as 'encouraging' (Quinney, 2005: 446). Second, there had also been concerns about possible inequality of access to the internet. In reality, this was not seen as a difficulty. While there was considerable variability in quality and quantity of student access to the internet while on placement, nonetheless students did not report insurmountable difficulties in accessing the forum, with some gaining access from home. Third, the main discussion themes were not the substantive placement learning themes that had been anticipated (for example, how to complete evidence sheets, or balance the workload). Instead they were about mutual support, in the form of relationship maintenance ('Hi everyone, hope your placements are all going OK, take care and see you on the link day'), or requests for general information about the course ('Hello everyone, does anyone know anything about the mental health and learning disability option in year 3?') (Quinney, 2005: 447). This ethos of mutual support shaped the use of the forum, with rather less evidence of 'deep learning' in relation to the placement experience.

Our second example of the use of online discussion groups to support practice learning comes from the work of Bushfield (2005) in the US. Here the online groups replaced an activity that had previously been occurring face-to-face. Students were divided into 'cluster groups', based on the geographical location of their placements. Previously these groups had met fortnightly, face-to-face, but student evaluation had been poor. Students reported a lack of clarity over the purpose of such meetings. They felt that they were an 'add-on', with the result that meetings were irregular and inconsistent. The online version was first run as a trial for some clusters, alongside clusters that continued to meet face-to-face. Bushfield (2005) reports some of the results as a comparison of the two approaches.

The aims of the online cluster groups were perhaps more ambitious than those in the Bournemouth model. They are listed as:

1 Addressing any problems or issues that arise in the field setting;
2 Fostering the integration of classroom and internship learning;
3 Enhancing the professional use of self; and
4 Fostering professional development and socialization. (Bushfield, 2005: 219)

The second of these aims seems to have been particularly important, with the author making a strong case for the significance of integrating class-room learning with practice learning whilst on placement – the theme with which we started this chapter. Bushfield suggests that 'web-based instruction may be particularly well-suited to integrative learning, because it allows for more time, review, and reflection on topics' (2005: 220). Certainly, the American model appears to direct students towards substan-tive learning much more strongly than does the Bournemouth model. Specifically, discussion topics are set by the instructor; students are required to input certain types of writing at certain stages (for example, case presen-tations and process recordings) and to comment on other people's inputs; students must respond to questions from the instructor and from fellow stu-dents. Most of this is done asynchronously, but there are also weekly 'live' sessions where the instructor is online to give real-time responses.

The online cluster model was evaluated in a similar way to the Bournemouth model. The main findings were as follows. First, students were enthusiastic about the online cluster groups, much more so than about the face-to-face alternative. Some specific advantages were mentioned:

• The flexibility of scheduling;
• The chance to take time to think about discussion topics;
• The opportunity for in-depth discussion (which might not have happened in a time-limited face-to-face session).

Second, students who said that they rarely felt confident enough to con-tribute verbally to face-to-face sessions reported that they were able to express themselves in the online clusters. Third, members of academic staff noted that the content of discussions was both richer and more focused than comparable classroom discussions (Bushfield, 2005).

The English and US approaches appear to be strongly contrasting. Whereas the English example is largely student-led and emphasises the value of mutual support, the American example is instructor-led and emphasises the substantive in-depth learning that was achieved. Perhaps surprisingly, neither example included in the discussion groups the students' agency-based practice teachers (England) or field instructors (USA). Given the central role that practice teachers/field instructors have in placement learning in both countries, this seems to be a major omission. Bushfield (2005) concludes by noting it and suggesting that there is a need to involve field instructors.

Learning with 'virtual' service users

No matter how good a student placement is, the opportunities for learning are limited to the 'cases' available at that particular time and place. Practice teachers may select suitable cases for students, or students may choose from an 'allocations' list. This process should be designed to facilitate learning, not just to meet the agency's need to get the work done. Sometimes there may be difficulty in finding the kind of work that will match a student's learning needs. One approach to solving this problem is to create 'virtual' case examples that students can access and learn from using ICT. We should acknowledge that such access is not limited to students on placement, and that university-based courses can also benefit from this approach. But we include the use of 'virtual' cases here, rather than in Chapter 6, because of the close links to practice learning.

Our first example comes from the Netherlands. Visser (1997) records how university teachers were making increasing use of case examples in a variety of social work courses, not just for illustration but in ways that involved students in analysing, reflecting and learning from cases. This led to the decision to create a database of cases, to systematise the process of learning from cases and create a 'library' of cases from which to learn. Cases were defined as having the following elements:

- A real life situation that could be met in practice placements
- A multi aspect client situation: psychosocial, financial, interpersonal or formal/legal
- The problem solving strategy has elements like: research, coordination, organisation and report
- The helping process can be of different nature: prevention, cure, etc. (Visser, 1997: 11).

The information on the database is very similar to the information collected in real-world client information systems such as those we have discussed in previous chapters. However, it can also include audio and video. Students are presented with a 'big basket' of unstructured and complex information. They must analyse the information and develop problem-solving strategies. Using ICT means that students can search the database for similar cases that may help. It also means that students can see one another's work and discuss cases online.

A second example comes once again from the University of Bournemouth in England. Quinney and colleagues (2008) describe an inter-professional approach to learning, using a 'virtual community' called 'Wessex Bay'. Wessex Bay is embedded in the Bournemouth VLE and can be accessed from on and off campus as an aid to placements, or university-based modules.

> By 'visiting' Wessex Bay, a seaside town with a rural hinterland and similar in that aspect to Bournemouth, and searching for individuals by name, keyword, or map location, they can visit the homes of residents and gather information about family structures, home conditions, the local community, and health and social care needs. A range of health and social work/care facilities are located here including a health centre, care home, day centres, and social services department, with information about the people accessing the services and the staff employed there. Relevant links are 'built-in' as appropriate, for example links to professional codes of conduct, legislation and agency policies. Scenarios have been developed in partnership with the service users and carers' advisory group, established to contribute to the design, delivery and assessment of the social work qualifying programme. (Quinney et al., 2008: 659–70)

Students have found the reality and the situatedness of Wessex Bay to be an aid to learning – case studies were no longer just something you read on paper. However, some struggled with using the IT, and the evaluation led to the conclusion that Wessex Bay should contain more detail about fewer families. But the main focus was on the inter-professional aspects, and here the learning was similar to that reported for face-to-face delivery. Students felt that inter-professional learning broke down prejudices and stereotypes, whilst highlighting how little some other professionals knew about the legal context of social work practice.

A third and final example comes from the USA (Zeman and Swanke, 2008). Here students were enrolled on a module that required them to make individual online contributions to the 'case files' of 'virtual consumers'. The whole class worked on six cases relating to domestic violence, child welfare, eldercare, substance abuse recovery and medical care. The class was divided into 'treatment teams' made up of therapists and case managers. Students were required to complete a 'consumer service plan', several sets of 'progress notes' and one 'systematic case review' – in their team role.

A distinctive feature of this module is that a primary aim was to improve students' ability to use ICT – *in their social work role*. This was not general ICT training, but was specifically targeted at students' ability to use the kind of ICT systems for case planning and recording that are in use in social work agencies. Whilst students were able to see and discuss one another's work, it would appear that the 'instructors' were seen as the experts. Certainly, Zeman and Swanke (2008) report that they, as instructors, were very active in giving feedback to students and in answering students' questions. Their evaluation of the module suggests that students became more confident about using ICT for social work practice, but that the '24/7 online environment' raised boundary difficulties for committed instructors who found themselves working evenings and weekends.

The significance of emotion

One of the significant differences between the examples we have considered is in their approach to understanding the feelings of students who may be using ICT while on placement. Whilst the account of the 'Placements Online' system at Bournemouth highlights the ways in which students used it to provide emotional support to one another, the other accounts do not refer to emotion at all.

Yet there is a growing awareness of the significance of emotion in learning that comes from attachment theory (Bowlby, 1988), brain research (Jensen, 2005), and from ideas about 'emotional intelligence' (Howe, 2008). MacFadden (2007) argues that, despite the image of ICT as being cold and impersonal, in fact emotion is significant in online communication and can be expressed in various ways. His model for web-based instruction (in relation to enhancing cultural competency) has three stages, as follows:

1 *Safety*. The aim is to create a safe learning environment where feelings of safety, support and acceptance are experienced by students.
2 *Challenge*. Students are challenged to think critically about their existing assumptions. This is likely to produce feelings of confusion, anxiety, and frustration.
3 *New thinking*. Finding resolutions is likely to produce 'Ah ha!' moments, with feelings of satisfaction and exhilaration. (MacFadden, 2007: 88)

The difficult feelings prompted by the second stage are seen as central to the learning process. In evaluating the module with students, MacFadden records that negative feelings (frustration, disconnection, etc.) outnumbered positive feelings (happy, free to 'speak') by two to one. Yet the significance of this is hard to interpret, given the centrality of difficult feelings in this model of learning and the normal tendency to remember negative emotions more easily. But students reported that they were able to communicate their emotions, sometimes using emoticons (e.g. ☺ – though seemingly gendered and more used by women) or using '???' for puzzlement, '!!!!' for enthusiasm, 'CAPS' for shouting (often considered bad e-manners!), 'hehe!' for humour or 'wow' for amazement. As with Quinney's students at Bournemouth, the online environment was not experienced as cold and impersonal, but 'as another means of making contact that was consistent with face-to-face transactions' (Quinney, 2005: 445). Warmth and humour were present, but students reported that their degree and style of online emotional expression depended on the pre-existing relationships between individuals and the size of the group (MacFadden, 2007).

Evaluating your Placement

Once placements are nearing completion, it is helpful to distinguish between two necessary strands of evaluation, whilst accepting that they are linked. The first strand is an evaluation of the placement itself – the nature of the learning opportunities, the quality of the teaching and supervision, and so on. The second strand is an evaluation of the student's performance and, in the UK, this is measured in main part against the National Occupational Standards for Social Work (NOS) (Topps UK, 2002). Each of these evaluative strands is being increasingly influenced by the use of ICT.

In the context of evaluating placements, a national quality assurance system for placement learning (QAPL) has recently been introduced in England (GSCC et al., 2009). This has three parts:

1 *An audit completed by university staff.* This collects basic data about the type of placement, and asks whether it provides an opportunity for students to meet each of the Key Roles in the NOS. It also asks whether it offers opportunities for meeting the GSCC code of practice, and for undertaking statutory social work tasks involving legal interventions.
2 *A student feedback form.* This covers all aspects of the student placement experience and gives the opportunity to raise any major concerns.
3 *A feedback form for the practice educator and/or supervisor.* This is a shorter form that asks for information about the setting up of the placement, the level of support from the university and agency colleagues, and the sources of evidence used in assessing the student.

It is likely that individual universities have been collecting similar data for some time. But this new system sets up a national database; with data uploaded by university staff in a prescribed format (an Access database is preferred). As we have seen with other databases, multiple aims and uses are built in. The claim is that the data may be used for workforce planning, but there are clearly questions that are designed to have a 'monitoring' role. What, for example, are we to make of question 15 in the university audit: 'Are daily placement fee arrangements clear?' What would be the consequence of answering: 'No'? It seems unlikely that anyone would do so! In fact, the extensive use of Yes/No boxes mean that, arguably, the data will be of limited use. For example, the question about whether or not there are opportunities for students to meet each of the key roles can only be answered 'Yes' or 'No'. Yet there is often considerable complexity here – the opportunities may vary with time, and much may depend on the ingenuity of individual practice teachers in creating such opportunities.

In the future the QAPL system is to become an integral part of the wider LeaRNS system (Skills for Care, 2010c) that was described earlier in the chapter. At the moment it is difficult to predict the impact that this use of ICT will have on placement provision and on practice learning.

When it comes to evaluating individual student performance on placement, several of the examples included in the previous section (Bushfield, 2005; Visser, 1997; Zeman and Swanke, 2008) have required students to submit assessed, placement-related assignments online. It is noticeable that none of these examples are from the UK. At the moment, individual UK universities have different ways of assessing student performance on placement against the national requirements. There is little evidence to suggest that online preparation or submission of such assessments is common. At the moment there does not appear to be any driver for the ICT-mediated national collation or monitoring of students' assessed performance on placement (as has happened with the quality assurance process for placements themselves).

Support for Learning after Qualification

It is clearly the case that, as with many professions, learning in social work does not stop at the point of initial qualification. The expectation that registered social workers should continue to learn and to develop is reinforced in England and Wales by the General Social Care Council.[3] The requirement for periodic re-registration is that social workers must 'complete either 90 hours or 15 days of study, training, courses, seminars, reading or other activities that could reasonably be expected to advance the

---

[3]See previous note regarding planned abolition of the General Social Care Council.

social worker's professional development or contribute to the development of the profession as a whole' (GSCC, 2007). In the remainder of this chapter we will consider two very contrasting ways in which ICT is used to support the continuing process of post-qualifying learning. In relation to both of these, there is considerable overlap and continuity with the role of ICT in supporting students on placement that we have considered above.

LeaRNS and the monitoring of formal post-qualifying study

The LeaRNS system 'to streamline the planning and delivery of work based learning for social workers at pre and post qualifying levels' (Skills for Care, 2009) is described earlier in the chapter. At the post-qualifying level, the intention is to create a database of all post-qualifying learning that is undertaken by individual social workers. Employers will then have easy access to the individual learning records of their employees, and staff will have access to the record of their professional development – one which will follow them from pre-qualifying student placements through the rest of their career.

LeaRNS is described as a 'modular system', where existing components can be added as desired and new ones added as they are developed. There is a module specifically designed to support the Newly Qualified Social Worker framework (NQSW) (Skills for Care, 2010b). This is an initiative designed to support social workers in their first year in practice. It acknowledges the need for a structured induction process, with access to good quality support and supervision, and opportunities for continuing professional development. But, as part of the induction process, the framework sets a series of 'outcome statements' in 12 areas of social work practice (e.g., communication, referral, assessment) that social workers are expected to attain by the time they reach the end of their first year. The LeaRNS system is designed to keep the record of social workers' achievement in each of these 12 areas, and more generally as they progress through the NQSW framework.

The LeaRNS system is primarily a tool for administrative monitoring of placements. It has a variety of overlapping uses, including placement planning, quality assurance reporting, payment of placement fees to agencies and tracking the professional development of individual social workers. But it does not contribute directly to the process of teaching and learning in practice settings. For that we need to turn to other uses of ICTs.

ICT supported 'Communities of Practice'

Communities of Practice (CoPs) were first mentioned in Chapter 4, as an example of the ways in which individual social workers may make use of

ICT. In this section we will explore the links between CoPs, ICT, and the concept of continuing professional development.

The term CoP originated in the 1990s with the work of Lave and Wenger (1991). It is used to describe a group of people who share a common interest. Members of a CoP interact with one another in ways that facilitate the sharing of relevant information: this leads to learning from one another and creates opportunities for personal and professional development. Whilst CoPs can exist in face-to-face settings such as a work canteen or common room (and, arguably, did so long before the term 'CoP' was invented), nonetheless with the advent of ICT-enabled communication methods CoPs have become increasingly significant because of their ability to bring together people who are otherwise separated in time and space.

Business organisations were the first to realise the potential of CoPs. Lesser and Storck (2001) argue that CoPs can improve organisation performance by, amongst other things, increasing the speed with which new employees learn the job and by reducing the amount of time spent 'reinventing the wheel'. Given these perceived advantages, and the commitment of the UK government to the use of ICT in service provision, it should not be surprising to find the government backing the development of CoPs in the public services. A prime example is the website *Communities of Practice for Local Government* (CoPfLG, 2010). As the website explains:

> Communities of practice for local government is a website that supports collaboration across local government and the public sector. It is a freely accessible resource that enables like-minded people to form online communities of practice, which are supported by collaboration tools that encourage knowledge sharing and learning from each others' experiences … The benefits of CoPs lie in providing a collaborative environment that connects people to other people, information and knowledge. Specifically CoPs can:
>
> - encourage the development and sharing of new ideas and strategies
> - support faster problem-solving
> - cut down on the duplication of effort
> - provide potentially endless access to expertise. (CoPfLG, 2010)

The service is provided by the Improvement and Development Agency for local government and a partnership is in place with the Improvement Service for local government in Scotland. Anyone can register and use the online tools to join an existing community or to create a new one and invite others to join. At the time of writing there are about 1,300 individual CoPs on the website.

CoPs and student social workers

CoPs may be highly relevant in social work education. Lave and Wenger's early work (1991) introduced the idea that newcomers become included in a CoP by way of 'legitimate peripheral participation'. At first newcomers observe, and then they may perform simple tasks, before moving on to become full members and to participate fully. This process is not primarily about gaining knowledge and skills; it is about learning how the CoP works, learning how to apply skills and knowledge in the specific local context, and becoming accepted within the CoP. Moore (2008) equates this process to the older concept of 'socialisation'. The process may be understood as occurring face-to-face (for example in the induction of new teachers: Moir and Hanson, 2008). For students on placement in social work agencies, Moore argues that ICT means that there are new opportunities 'to connect field educators, faculty, community practitioners, clients and students. Online CoPs may allow newcomers to share their ideas and experiences with seasoned veteran workers, who in turn mentor and guide others through the process of legitimate peripheral participation' (Moore, 2008: 598).

CoPs and continuing professional development

Implicit in the preceding section is the idea that newcomers are interacting with established members of the CoP who themselves are engaged in sharing information with others and, in the process, learning and developing. Two research studies have sought to evaluate the operation of CoPs in social work and, amongst other objectives, to examine the extent to which this process actually happens.

The first study (Cook-Craig and Sabah, 2009) is of 18 CoPs that were set up by the Israeli Ministry for Social Affairs to facilitate inter-organisational learning amongst 'human service providers'. Community topics were a mix of the 'professional' and the 'managerial'. The first finding was that most people used the CoPs to access information, but sometimes without indicating their presence and certainly without contributing any 'posts' (sometimes known as 'lurking', although reading but not posting online is not necessarily a negative feature). Only a small number of people were active in the communities. As we noted in Chapter 4, this is consistent with other studies on the use of online discussion forums of various types. It is not entirely clear whether this reflects a problem that is peculiar to or (perhaps more likely), exacerbated by the online nature of the communication.

After all, face-to-face groups are known to have similar characteristics. A second finding was that many of the practitioners struggled to find the time to reflect on their practice using the CoPs. Cook-Craig and Sabah (2009) argue that organisational structures and policies must change so as to allow time for knowledge dissemination. Finally, they note the absence of services users from the CoPs. They argue that more research is needed into the differences that might occur in any future CoPs that include service users. This would be a significant development and one that would reflect a distinctive social work contribution to the development of CoPs. In Chapter 3 we noted the creation of the Social Work Education Participation (SWEP) website at http://www.socialworkeducation.org.uk/. At this site both service user organisations and Higher Education Institutions can post information about their activities in relation to social work education, and this is the closest that we are aware of to a CoP that includes service users.

The second study (LaMendola et al., 2009) evaluates a networked approach to learning amongst social workers in a large, rural local authority in Scotland. This time the communication was not exclusively online, but a 'blended' design that also included face-to-face meetings. In this context, participants reported that they felt that the online communication was a supplement to the face-to-face meetings that they found the most beneficial. In particular, they talked about the difficulty of developing trust in the early stages of the group when communication was online, in text-only form. 'Just typing' was seen as a much reduced form of communication. It is noticeable that similar views were not expressed in the Israeli study where the only communication was online. However, the participants in the Scottish study matched those in the Israeli study exactly insofar as they felt that it was 'very difficult to find time to contribute to an online discussion because of the demands of an already excessive workload' (LaMendola et al., 2009: 719). Despite the fact that managers had approved a specific amount of time each week for them to spend on it, participants found that the reality of front line practice is that there are always more pressing things to do.

We referred in the Introduction to our intention to walk a balancing act throughout this book, and to challenge readers to ask why ICT is used and how this affects and impacts on practice and the experience of people who use services. We have sought to facilitate a practical knowledge, but with a more demanding sense of 'practical' than is often assumed. Finally, we have aspired to support readers in pushing ahead from the basis provided in this book.

Taking it further

Exercise 7.1

Garrison and Vaughan (2008: 5) define blended learning as 'the thoughtful fusion of face-to-face and online learning experiences'. Read the introduction to their book, and also the article by LaMendola and others (2009), quoted at the end of this chapter.

Set up a group session in your agency, jointly with practitioners, and review the possibilities for a blended learning approach to your placement experience. Do you find Garrison and Vaughan's Community of Inquiry Framework helpful?

For more about the LeaRNS system visit the Skills for Care website at http://www.skillsforcare.org.uk/socialwork/LeaRNS/LeaRNSnew.aspx

For information about the virtual community of Wessex Bay visit http://www.bournemouth.ac.uk/hsc/wessexbay.html

For more about Communities of Practice in local government visit http://www.communities.idea.gov.uk/welcome.do

References

Action on Rights for Children (2010) 'Consent to information sharing', *Action on Rights for Children website*, http://www.arch-ed.org/issues/databases/consent_to_information_sharing.htm (accessed 5 February 2010).

acto (2010) 'Code of ethics', *acto website*, http://acto-uk.org/codeofethics.htm (accessed 12 May 2010).

Anderson, R., Brown, I., Dowty, T., Inglesant, P., Heath, W. and Sasse, A. (2009) 'Database state: A report commissioned by the Joseph Rowntree Reform Trust – Executive Summary', *jrrt website*, http://www.jrrt.org.uk/uploads/Database%20State%20-%20Executive%20Summary.pdf (accessed 21 January 2010).

Anderson, S., Allen, P., Peckham, S. and Goodwin, N. (2008) 'Asking the right questions: Scoping studies in the commissioning of research on the organisation and delivery of health services', *Health Research Policy and Systems*, 6(7): doi:10.1186/1478-4505-6-7-

Ball, K., Lyon, D., Wood, D., Norris, C. and Raab, C. (2006) *A Report on the Surveillance Society for the Information Commissioner by the Surveillance Studies Network*. London: The Information Commissioner.

BASW (2002) *The Code of Ethics for Social Work*. Birmingham: BASW.

Bayley, M. (1973) *Mental Handicap and Community Care*. London: Routledge and Kegan Paul.

Beatbullying (2009) 'Virtual violence: Protecting children from cyberbullying', *Beatbullying website*, http://www.beatbullying.org/pdfs/Virtual%20Violence%20-%20Protecting%20Children%20from%20Cyberbullying.pdf (accessed 12 May 2010).

Beech, R. and Roberts, D. (2008) 'Assistive technology and older people', *SCIE website – briefing paper 28*, http://www.scie.org.uk/publications/briefings/briefing28/ (accessed 13 March 2010).

Bell, M., Shaw, I., Sinclair, I., Sloper, P. and Rafferty, J. (2007) *The Integrated Children's System: An Evaluation of the Practice, Process and Consequences of the ICS in Councils with Social Services Responsibilities (Full Report). A Report to Department for Education and Skills/Welsh Assembly Government*. York: University of York.

Blum, S. (2009) *My Word! Plagiarism and College Culture*. Ithaca, NY: Cornell University Press.

Bowlby, J. (1988) *A Secure Base: Clinical Applications of Attachment Theory*. London: Routledge.

Branfield, F. (2009) *SCIE Report 29: Developing User Involvement in Social Work Education*. London: SCIE.

Brotsky, S. and Giles, D. (2007) 'Inside the pro-ana community', *Eating Disorder*, 15(2): 93–109.

Buchanan, J., Wilson, S.T. and Gopal, N. (2008) 'A cross cultural learning environment for students to explore the issue of racism: A case study involving the UK, USA and SA', *Social Work Education*, 27(6): 671–682.

Burgess, E. (1923) 'The interdependence of sociology and social work', *Journal of Social Forces*, 1(4): 366–370.

Burgess, E. (1927) 'The contribution of sociology to family social work', *The Family*, Oct: 191–193.

Burgess, E. (1928) 'What social case records should contain to be useful for socio-logical interpretation', *Social Forces*, 6(4): 524–532.

Bushfield, S. (2005) 'Field clusters online', *Journal of Technology in Human Services*, 23(2&3): 215–227.

Cabinet Office (1998) *Our Information Age: The Government's Vision*. London: Cabinet Office.

Cabinet Office (2000) *E-Government: A Strategic Framework for Public Services in the Information Age*. London: Cabinet Office.

Cafcass (2010) 'Cafcass Young Peer Mentors', *Cafcass website*, http://www.cafcass.gov.uk/cafcass_and_you/peer_mentoring.aspx (accessed 23 March 2010).

Carr, D. (2008) 'Learning and the virtual world', in N. Selwyn (ed.) *Education 2.0? Designing the web for teaching and learning Tlrp website*, http://www.tlrp.org/pub/documents/TELcomm.pdf (accessed 10 May 2010).

Carrington, A. and Green, I. (2007) 'Just in time teaching revisited: Using e-assessment and rapid e-learning to empower face to face teaching', *ICT: Providing choices for learners and learning. Proceedings of ascilite conference Singapore 2007*, http://www.ascilite.org.au/conferences/singapore07/procs/carrington-poster.pdf (accessed 12 May 2010).

Carvel, J. (2004) 'All eyes on the child', *Guardian online*, http://www.guardian.co.uk/society/2004/may/19/childrenservices 3 (accessed 12 October 2010).

Castells, M. (2001) *The Internet Galaxy*. Oxford: Oxford University Press.

Clapton, J. and Rutter, D. and Sharif, N. (2009) *SCIE Systematic Mapping Guidance*. London: Social Care Institute for Excellence.

Cleaver, D. (2005) 'Briefing paper 8: English pilots ICS IT systems technical report', *Every Child Matters website*, http://www.dcsf.gov.uk/everychildmatters/safeguardingandsocialcare/integratedchildrenssystem/icstechnicalresources/tech/ (accessed 29 January 2010).

Coleman, N. (2009) 'This is the modern world! Working in a social services contact centre', in Harris, J. and White, V. (eds), *Modernising Social Work: Critical Considerations*, pp. 31–50. Bristol: Policy Press.

Cook-Craig, P. and Sabah, Y. (2009) 'The role of virtual communities of practice in supporting collaborative learning among social workers', *British Journal of Social Work*, 39(4): 725–739.

Cooner, T. (2004) 'Preparing for ICT enhanced practice learning opportunities in 2010 – a speculative view', *Social Work Education*, 23(6): 731–744.

Cooner, T.S. (2010) 'Creating opportunities for students in large cohorts to reflect in and on practice: Lessons learnt from a formative evaluation of students' experiences of a technology-enhanced blended learning design', *British Journal of Educational Technology*, 41(2): 271–286.

CoPfLG (2010) 'Communities of Practice for Local Government', *Communities of Practice for Local Government website*, http://www.communities.idea.gov.uk/welcome.do (accessed 18 March 2010).

Coren, E. and Fisher, M. (2006) 'The conduct of systematic research reviews for SCIE knowledge reviews', *SCIE website*, http://www.scie.org.uk/publications/researchresources/rr01.asp (accessed 10 May 2010).

Couldry, N. (2000) 'The digital divide', in Gauntlett, D. and Horsley, R. (eds), *Web Studies*, (2nd edn), pp. 185–194. London: Arnold.

Crook, C. (2008) 'What are web 2.0 technologies, and why do they matter?', in N. Selwyn (ed.) *Education 2.0? Designing the web for teaching and learning*, *Tlrp website*, http://www.tlrp.org/pub/documents/TELcomm.pdf (accessed 10 May 2010).

Daily Strength (2009) 'Daily strength', *Daily Strength website*, http://www.dailystrength.org/ (accessed 23 October 2009).

Daly, E. and Ballantyne, N. (2009) 'Retelling the past using new technologies: A case study into the digitization of social work heritage material and the creation of a virtual exhibition', *Journal of Technology in Human Services*, 27(1): 44–56.

Darr, A. and Warhurst, C. (2008) 'Assumptions, assertions and the need for evidence: Debugging debates about knowledge workers', *Current Sociology*, 56(1): 25–45.

Department for Children, Schools and Families (2009a) 'About the integrated children's system', *Every Child Matters website*, http://www.dcsf.gov.uk/everychildmatters/safeguardingandsocialcare/integratedchildrenssystem/abouttheintegratedchildrenssystem/about/ (accessed 25 August 2009).

Department for Children, Schools and Families (2009b) 'ContactPoint', *Every Child Matters website*, http://www.dcsf.gov.uk/everychildmatters/strategy/deliveringservices1/contactpoint/contactpoint/ (accessed 21 August 2009).

Department for Children, Schools and Families (2009c) *ContactPoint: Lessons Learned From the Early Adopters Phase*. London: Department for Children, Schools and Families.

Department for Children, Schools and Families (2009d) 'E-enablement of the Common Assessment Framework (CAF): National eCAF', *Every Child Matters website*, http://www.dcsf.gov.uk/everychildmatters/strategy/deliveringservices1/caf/ecaf/ecaf/ (accessed 25 August 2009).

Department for Children, Schools and Families (2009e) 'The Common Assessment Framework', *Every Child Matters website*, http://www.dcsf.gov.uk/everychildmatters/strategy/deliveringservices1/caf/cafframework/ (accessed 25 August 2009).

Department of Health (2000) *Framework for the Assessment of Children in Need and their Families*. London: The Stationery Office.

Department of Health (2002) 'Single Assessment Process', *Department of Health website*, http://www.dh.gov.uk/en/SocialCare/Chargingandassessment/SingleAssessmentProcess/DH_079509#_1 (accessed 19 October 2009).

Department of Health (2007) 'What is social work: The role', *Department of Health*, http://www.socialworkandcare.co.uk/socialwork/what/index.asp (accessed 24 April 2007).

Department of Health (2009) 'Common Assessment Framework for Adults demonstrator site programme: Overview of Phase 1 sites', *Department of Health website*, http://www.dh.gov.uk/en/Publicationsandstatistics/Publications/PublicationsPolicyAndGuidance/DH_099703 (accessed 23 February 2010).

Depression and Bipolar Support Alliance (2009) 'DBSA online support groups', *Depression and Bipolar Support Alliance website*, http://www.dbsalliance.org/site/PageServer?pagename=support_OSGnocomponent (accessed 23 October 2009).

DivorceSource (2009) 'Online divorce support forums', *DivorceSource website*, http://www.divorcesource.com/wwwboard/bulletin.html (accessed 23 October 2009).

Donovan, K. and Saxon, L. (2009) 'eCPD Programme – Enhanced Learning', *eCPD National Launch Conference – ALT website*, http://repository.alt.ac.uk/736/ (accessed 10 May 2010).

Dowty, T. and Korff, D. (2009) 'Protecting the virtual child – the law and children's consent to sharing personal data', *ARCH website*, http://www.archrights.org.uk/docs/NYA(4)arch_16.2.0[2].pdf (accessed 12 May 2010).

Ehlers, U. (2007) 'A new pathway for e-learning: From distribution to collaboration and competence in e-learning', *AACE Journal*, 16(2): 187–202.

ePPI-Centre (2010) 'User driven evidence informed policy and practice', *ePPI-Centre website*, http://eppi.ioe.ac.uk/cms/Default.aspx?tabid=65 (accessed 10 May 2010).

Evans, T. and Harris, J. (2004) 'Street level bureaucracy, social work and the (exaggerated) death of discretion', *British Journal of Social Work*, 34(6): 871–895.

Families Need Fathers (2009) 'Familes Need Fathers', *Families Need Fathers website*, http://www.fnf.org.uk/home (accessed 25 October 2009).

Felleman, D. (2005) 'Pragmatism and clinical practices', *Journal of Social Work Values and Ethics website*, 2. [Online.] Available at http://www.socialworker.com/jswve/content/view/14/34/ (accessed 1 June 2009).

Ferguson, H. (2005) 'Working with violence, the emotions and the psycho-social dynamics of child protection: Reflections on the Victoria Climbié case', *Social Work Education*, 24(7): 781–795.

Finn, J. (2008) 'Technology and practice: Micro-practice', in Mizrahi, T. and Davis, L. (eds), *Encyclopedia of Social Work*, pp. 215–216. New York: NASW Press and Oxford University Press.

Fujitsu (2009) 'Fujitsu sign £25 million deal with Cafcass for public sector Flex', *Fujitsu press release*, http://www.fujitsu.com/uk/news/pr/fs_20080320.html (accessed 18 September 2009).

GamAid (2009) 'GamAid Forum', *GamAid online forum*, http://www.gamaid.com/forum/default.asp (accessed 23 October 2009).

Garrett, P. (2005) 'Social work's "electronic turn": Notes on the deployment of information and communication technologies in social work with children and families', *Critical Social Policy*, 25(4): 529–553.

Garrett, P. (2009) *'Transforming' Children's Services? Social Work, Neoliberalism and the 'Modern' World*. Maidenhead: McGraw Hill/OUP.

Garrison, D.R. and Vaughan, N.D. (2008) *Blended Learning in Higher Education: Framework, Principles and Guidelines*. San Francisco: Jossey-Bass.

Gauntlett, D. (2004) 'Web studies: What's new?', in Gauntlett, D. and Horsley, R. (eds), *Web Studies* (2nd edn), pp. 3–23. London: Arnold.

Glastonbury, B. (1985) *Computers in Social Work*. Basingstoke: Macmillan.

GROWW (2009) 'Grief Recovery Online for All Bereaved', *GROWW website*, http://www.groww.org/ (accessed 23 October 2009).

GSCC (2007) 'Guidance notes on how to renew your registration', *GSCC website*, http://www.gscc.org.uk/NR/rdonlyres/ED46DE70-6579-4170-BE08-0708C76 DAF56/0/82459COIGSCCGuidance.pdf (accessed 16 March 2010).

GSCC, CWDC and Skills for Care (2009) 'Quality assurance for practice learning: Quality assurance benchmark statement and guidance on the monitoring of social work practice learning opportunities (QAPL)', *Skills for Care website*, http://www. skillsforcare.org.uk/socialwork/practiceplacements/sw_national_projects.aspx (accessed 13 March 2010).

Hall, C. (1997) *Social Work As Narrative: Storytelling and Persuasion in Professional Texts.* Aldershot: Ashgate.

Hanson, J., Osipovic, D. and Percival, J. (2009) 'Making sense of sensors: Older people's and professional caregivers' attitudes towards telecare', in Loader, B., Hardey, M. and Keeble, L. (eds), *Digital Welfare for the Third Age: Health and Social Care Informatics for Older People*, pp. 91–111. London: Routledge.

Hardey, M. (2002) '"The story of my illness": Personal accounts of illness on the internet', *Health*, 6(1): 31–46.

Hardey, M. and Loader, B. (2009) 'The informatization of welfare: Older people and the role of digital services', *British Journal of Social Work*, 39(4): 657–669.

Hartswood, M., Proctor, R., Slack, R., Voß, A., Büscher, M., Rouncefield, M. and Rouchy, P. (2002) 'Co-realisation: Towards a principled synthesis of ethnomethodology and participatory design', *Scandinavian Journal of Information Systems*, 14(2): 9–30.

Heath, C. and Luff, P. (2000) *Technology in Action.* Cambridge: Cambridge University Press.

Heaton, J., Sloper, P. and Shah, R. (2005) 'Families' experience of caring for technology-dependent children: A temporal perspective', *Health and Social Care in the Community*, 13(5): 441–450.

Heaton, J., Noyes, J., Sloper, P. and Shah, R. (2006) 'Sleep disruption and technology dependent children', *Children and Society*, 20(3): 196–208.

Henman, P. and Adler, M. (2003) 'Information technology and the governance of social security', *Critical Social Policy*, 23(2): 139–164.

Hill, A. (2010) *Working in Statutory Contexts.* Cambridge: Polity Press.

House of Thin (2009) 'House of thin', *House of Thin – pro-anorexia website*, http:// www.houseofthin.com/ (accessed 25 October 2009).

Howe, D. (1996) 'Surface and depth in social work practice', in Parton, N. (ed.), *Social Theory, Social Change and Social Work*, pp. 77–87. London: Routledge.

Howe, D. (2008) *The Emotionally Intelligent Social Worker.* Basingstoke: Palgrave Macmillan.

Hucklesby, A. (2008) 'Vehicles of desistance? The impact of electronically monitored curfew orders', *Criminology and Criminal Justice*, 8(1): 51–71.

Hudson, J. (2002) 'Digitising the structures of government: The UK's information age government agenda', *Policy & Politics*, 30(4): 515–531.

IFSW (2005) 'Ethics in social work: Statement of principles', *IFSW website*, http:// www.ifsw.org/f38000032.html (accessed 23 December 2009).

International Federation of Social Workers (2000) 'Definition of social work', *IFSW website*, http://www.ifsw.org/f38000138.html (accessed 21 August 2009).

ITU (2009) 'Online child protection guidelines', *ITU website*, http://www.itu.int/osg/csd/cybersecurity/gca/cop/guidelines/index.html (accessed 12 May 2010).

Ixer, G. (2009) 'Changes to the European Computer Driving Licence (ECDL) requirement to take effect from 1st September 2009', *GSCC website*, http://www.gscc.org.uk/NR/rdonlyres/FD8A3CCF-AF21-472E-A3DA-7D0349478869/0/ECDLLetter_to_HEIs.pdf (accessed 12 May 2010).

Jensen, E. (2005) *Teaching With the Brain in Mind* (2nd edn). Alexandria, VA: Association for Supervision and Curriculum Development.

Jones, G. and Stokes, A. (2009) *Online Counselling: A Handbook for Practitioners*. London: Palgrave Macmillan.

Jones, K., Cooper, B. and Ferguson, H. (2008) 'Introducing critical best practice in social work', in Jones, K., Cooper, B. and Ferguson, H. (eds), *Best Practice in Social Work: Critical Perspectives*, pp. 1–11. Basingstoke: Palgrave Macmillan.

Jones, R. (2000) 'Digital rule: Punishment, control and technology', *Punishment Society*, 2(1): 5–22.

JSTOR (2010) 'Trusted archives for scholarship', *JSTOR website*, http://www.jstor.org/?cookieSet=1 (accessed 10 May 2010).

Kent County Council (2009) 'Self assessment', *Kent County Council online*, http://www.kent.gov.uk/SocialCare/adults-and-older-people/self-assessment/default.htm (accessed 21 August 2009).

Kitchen, H. (2002) 'The Tri Council on cyberspace: Insights, oversights and extrapolations', in W. C. van den Hoonaard (ed.), *Walking the Tightrope: Ethical Issues for Qualitative Researchers*. Toronto: University of Toronto Press.

Kooth (2009) 'Free online advice for young people', *Kooth website*, https://www.kooth.com/index.php (accessed 25 October 2009).

LaMendola, W., Ballantyne, N. and Daly, E. (2009) 'Practitioner networks: Professional learning in the twenty-first century', *British Journal of Social Work*, 39(4): 710–724.

Landau, R., Werner, S., Auslander, G., Shoval, N. and Heinik, J. (2009) 'Attitudes of family and professional care-givers towards the use of GPS for tracking patients with dementia: An exploratory study', *British Journal of Social Work*, 39(4): 670–692.

Langan, J. (2009) 'Mental health, risk communication and data quality in the electronic age', *British Journal of Social Work*, 39(3): 467–487.

Laurent, V. (2008) 'ICT and social work: A question of identities?', in Fischer-Hubner, S., Dubquenoy, P., Zuccato, A. and Martucci, A. (eds), *The Future of Identity in the Information Society*, pp. 375–386 (International Federation for Information Processing, Vol. 262). Boston: Springer.

Lave, J. and Wenger, E. (1991) *Situated Learning: Legitimate Peripheral Participation*. Cambridge: Cambridge University Press.

Lax, S. (2004) 'The internet and democrary', in Gauntlett, D. and Horsley, R. (eds), *Web Studies* (2nd edn), pp. 217–229. London: Arnold.

Lesser, E. and Storck, J. (2001) 'Communities of practice and organizational performance', *IBM Systems Journal*, 40(4): 831–841.

Lombard, D. (2010) 'Social work academic wants to see placement system scrapped', *Community Care website*, http://www.communitycare.co.uk/Articles/2010/02/19/113857/ social-work-academic-spells-out-radical-degree-changes.htm (accessed 9 March 2010).

Lorenz, W. (2007) 'Practising history: Memory and contemporary professional practice', *International Social Work*, 50(5): 597–612.

Lunt, N., Shaw, I. and Mitchell, F. (2009) 'Practitioner research in CHILDREN 1st: Cohorts, networks and systems', *Institute for Research and Innovation in the Social Services website*, http://www.iriss.org.uk/files/Children1stEvaluation_Final.pdf (accessed 1 August 2009).

MacFadden, R. (2007) 'The forgotten dimension in learning: Incorporating emotion into web-based education', *Journal of Technology in Human Services*, 25(1/2): 85–101.

Mathieson, S. (2009) 'Between blue sky and blueprints', *Guardian online*, http://www.smarthealthcare.com/conservative-plans-stephen-obrien-national-programme-19aug09 (accessed 21 August 2009).

MDJunction (2009) 'MDJunction', *MDJunction website*, http://www.mdjunction.com/support-groups (accessed 23 October 2009).

Mickel, A. and Miskelly, B. (2009) 'Telecare and assistive technology fits in to the personalisation agenda', *CommunityCare.co.uk*, http://www.communitycare.co.uk/Articles/2009/06/08/111762/telecare-and-assistive Technology-fits-in-to-the-personalisation.htm (accessed 12 October 2009).

Milner, J. and O'Byrne, P. (2002) 'Assessment and planning', in Adams, R., Dominelli, L. and Payne, M. (eds), *Critical Practice in Social Work*, pp. 261–268. Basingstoke: Palgrave Macmillan.

Mitchell, W. and Sloper, P. (2008) 'Evaluation of the pilot programme of the integrated children's system: The disability study', *University of York Social Policy Research Unit website*, http://www.york.ac.uk/inst/spru/pubs/pdf/ics.pdf (accessed 13 March 2010).

Moir, E. and Hanson, S. (2008) 'A learning community for teacher induction', in Kincheloe, J., Beck, C., Freese, A., Kosnik, C., Samaras, A. and Steinburg, S. (eds), *Learning Communities in Practice*, pp. 155–163. Dordrecht, Netherlands: Springer.

Moore, B. (2008) 'Using technology to promote communities of practice (CoP) in social work education', *Social Work Education: The International Journal*, 27(6): 592–600.

Murphy, L., Parnass, P., Mitchell, D.L., Hallett, R., Cayley, P. and Seagram, S. (2009) 'Client satisfaction and outcome comparisons of online and face-to-face counselling methods', *British Journal of Social Work*, 39(4): 627–640.

Murray, D. and Aspinall, A. (2006) *Getting IT: Using Information Technology to Empower People with Communication Difficulties*. London: Jessica Kingsley.

NASW (2005) 'Standards for technology and social work practice', *NASW website*, http://www.naswdc.org/practice/default.asp (accessed 30 March 2010).

NASW (2008) 'Code of Ethics of the National Association of Social Workers', *NASW website*, http://www.socialworkers.org/pubs/code/code.asp (accessed 23 December 2009).

National Autistic Society (2009) 'National Autistic Society', *National Autistic Society website*, http://www.nas.org.uk/ (accessed 25 October 2009).

Nellis, M. (1991) 'The electronic monitoring of offenders in England and Wales: Recent developments and future prospects', *British Journal of Criminology*, 31(2): 165–185.

Nellis, M. (2003) 'News media, popular culture and the electronic monitoring of offenders in England and Wales', *Howard Journal of Criminal Justice*, 42(1): 1–31.

Nellis, M. (2005) 'Out of this world: The advent of the satellite tracking of offenders in England and Wales', *Howard Journal of Criminal Justice*, 44(2): 125–150.

New Media Consortium and EDUCAUSE Learning Initiative (2010) 'The 2010 Horizon report', *NMC website*, http://www.nmc.org/pdf/2010-Horizon-Report. pdf (accessed April 2010).

NHS Choices (2009) 'Technology for carers', *NHS Choices website*, http://www.nhs. uk/carersdirect/carerslives/pages/technologyforcarers.aspx (accessed 25 August 2009).

NHS London (2009) 'About eSAP', *NHS London website,* http://www.london.nhs. uk/lpfit/support-for-trusts/publications/about-esap (accessed 25 August 2009).

Nix, I. (2010) 'Technology-enhanced learning for social work education and practice', in Matthews, S., McCormick, M., Morgan, A. and Seden, J. (eds), *Professional Development in Social Work: Complex Issues in Practice*, pp. 150–156. London: Routledge.

Norris, P. (2001) *Digital Divide: Civic Engagement, Information Poverty, and the Internet Worldwide*. Cambridge: Cambridge University Press.

O'Donnell, D. and Henriksen, L. (2002) 'Philosophical foundations for a critical evaluation of the social impact of ICT', *Journal of Information Technology*, 17: 89–99.

Orgad, S. (2004) 'Help yourself: The world wide web as a self-help agora', in Gauntlett, D. and Horsley, R. (eds), *Web Studies* (2nd edn), pp. 147–157. London: Arnold.

Parton, N. (2008a) 'Towards the preventative-surveillance state: The current changes in children's services in England', in Burns, K. and Lynch, D. (eds), *Child Protection and Welfare Social Work: Contemporary Themes and Practice Perspectives*, pp. 75–89. Dublin: A & A Farmar.

Parton, N. (2008b) 'Changes in the form of knowledge in social work: from the "social" to the "Informational"?', *British Journal of Social Work*, 38(2): 253–269.

Peckover, S., White, S. and Hall, C. (2008) 'Making and managing electronic children: E-assessment in child welfare', *Information, Communication & Society,* 11(3): 375–394.

Penna, S. (2005) 'The Children Act 2004: Child protection and social surveillance', *Journal of Social Welfare and Family Law*, 27(2): 143–157.

Pinnock, H., Slack, R., Pagliari, C., Price, D. and Sheikh, A. (2006) 'Professional and patient attitudes to using mobile phone technology to monitor asthma: Questionnaire survey', *Primary Care Respiratory Journal*, 15(4): 237–245.

Pithouse, A., Hall, C., Peckover, S. and White, S. (2009) 'A Tale of two CAFs: The impact of the electronic common assessment framework', *British Journal of Social Work*, 39(4): 599–612.

Quality Assurance Agency (2000) 'Subject benchmark statement: Social policy and administration and social work', *Quality Assurance Agency website*, http://www.qaa. ac.uk/academicinfrastructure/benchmark/honours/socialwork.pdf (accessed 1 August 2009).

Quayle, E., Loof, L. and Palmer, T. (2008) 'Child pornography and sexual exploitation of children online', *ECPAT network website*, http://www.childcentre.info/public/ Thematic_Paper_ICTPsy_ENG.pdf (accessed 12 May 2010).

Quinney, A. (2005) 'Placements online: Student experiences of a website to support learning in practice settings', *Social Work Education,* 24(4): 439–450.

Quinney, A., Hutchings, M. and Scammell, J. (2008) 'Student and staff experiences of using a virtual community, Wessex Bay, to support interprofessional learning: Messages for collaborative practice', *Social Work Education,* 27(6): 658–664.

Rafferty, J. and Waldman, J. (2003) 'Building capacity to support the social work degree: A scoping study for the Department of Health elearning steering group',

DoH website, http://www.dh.gov.uk/en/Publicationsandstatistics/Publications/PublicationsPolicyAndGuidance/DH_4120184 (accessed 9 March 2010).

Rafferty, J. and Waldman, J. (2006) 'Fit for virtual social work practice?', *Journal of Technology in Human Services,* 24(2/3): 1–22.

Richardson, A. and Cherry, E. (2005) 'Anorexia as a lifestyle: Agency through pro-anorexia websites', Paper presented at the annual meeting of the American Sociological Association, Marriott Hotel, Loews Philadelphia Hotel, Philadelphia, PA, 12 August. http://www.allacademic.com//meta/p_mla_apa_research_citation/0/2/2/9/9/pages22991/p22991-1.php (accessed 1 May 2010).

Rockinson-Szapkiw, A.J. and Walker, V.L. (2009) 'Web 2.0 technologies: Facilitating interaction in an online human services counselling course', *Journal of Technology in Human Services,* 27(3): 175–193.

Rowntree, N. (2009) 'Joint working: ContactPoint – The verdict so far', *Children and Young People Now website,* http://www.cypnow.co.uk/news/showcase/943670/ (accessed April 2010).

Rye, S.A. and Zubaidah, I. (2008) 'Distance education and the complexity of accessing the Internet', *Open Learning: The Journal of Open and Distance Learning,* 23(2): 95–102.

Sapey, B. (1997) 'Social work tomorrow: Towards a critical understanding of technology in social work', *British Journal of Social Work,* 27(6): 803–814.

Schön, D. (1983) *The Reflective Practitioner: How Professionals Think in Action.* New York: Basic Books.

Schwandt, T. (1997) 'Evaluation as practical hermeneutics', *Evaluation,* 3(1): 69–83.

SCIE (2006) 'E-Readiness in the social care sector: Building capacity for e-learning', *Social Care Institute for Excellence website,* http://www.scie.org.uk/publications/consultation/readiness.pdf (accessed 1 August 2009).

Seebohm, F. (1968) *Report of the Committee on Local Authority and Allied Personal Social Services.* London: HMSO.

Selwyn, N. (ed.) (2008) 'Education 2.0? Designing the web for teaching and learning. Commentary by the Technology Enhanced Learning phase of the Teaching and Learning Research Programme (TLRP)', *TLRP website,* http://www.tlrp.org/pub/documents/TELcomm.pdf (accessed 10 May 2010).

Shaping Our Lives (2010) 'Shaping our lives: National user network', *Shaping Our Lives website,* http://www.shapingourlives.org.uk/index.html (accessed 5 January 2010).

Shaw, I. and Clayden, J. (2009) 'Technology and professional practice: Reflections on the Integrated Children's System', *Journal of Children's Services,* 4(4): 15–27.

Shaw, I., Morris, K. and Edwards, A. (2009a) 'Technology, social services and organizational innovation *or* How great expectations in London and Cardiff are dashed in Lowestoft and Cymtyrch', *Journal of Social Work Practice,* 23(4): 383–400.

Shaw, I., Bell, M., Sinclair, I., Sloper, P., Mitchell, W., Dyson, P., Clayden, J. and Rafferty, J. (2009b) 'An exemplary scheme? An evaluation of the Integrated Children's System', *British Journal of Social Work,* 39(4): 613–626.

Sherraden, M. and Sherraden, M. (2000) 'Asset building: Integrating research, education and practice', *Advances in Social Work,* 1(1): 61–77.

Skills for Care (2009) 'LeaRNS FAQs', *Skills for Care website,* http://www.skillsforcare.org.uk/socialwork/LeaRNS/LeaRNSnew.aspx (accessed 9 March 2010).

Skills for Care (2010a) 'LeaRNS briefing 6', *Skills for Care website*, http://www.skills-forcare.org.uk/socialwork/LeaRNS/LeaRNSnew.aspx (accessed 9 March 2010).

Skills for Care (2010b) 'Newly qualified social worker framework', *Skills for Care website*, http://www.skillsforcare.org.uk/socialwork/NewlyQualifiedSocialWorker/NewlyQualifiedSocialWorker.aspx (accessed 17 March 2010).

Skills for Care (2010c) 'Welcome to LeaRNS', *Skills for Care website*, http://www.skillsforcare.org.uk/socialwork/LeaRNS/LeaRNSnew.aspx (accessed 9 March 2010).

Smith, A., Schlozman, K., Verba, S. and Brady, H. (2009) 'The internet and civic engagement', *www.pewinternet.org*, http://www.pewinternet.org/Reports/2009/15-The-Internet-and-Civic-Engagement (accessed 5 January 2010).

Social Care Institute for Excellence (2009) *At a Glance 19: Building User and Carer Involvement in Social Work Education*. London: SCIE.

Social Care Institute for Excellence (2010) 'About SCIE', *SCIE website,* http://www.scie.org.uk/about/index.asp (accessed 6 January 2010).

Social Work Taskforce (2009a) *Final Report of the Social Work Task Force*. London: Department for Children, Schools and Families.

Social Work Taskforce (2009b) *First Report of the Social Work Task Force*. London: Department for Children, Schools and Families.

Sweney, M. (2009) 'ASA's Christopher Graham set to become information commissioner', *Guardian online*, http://www.guardian.co.uk/media/2009/jan/13/asa-christopher-graham-to-become-information-commissioner (accessed 13 January 2009).

Taylor, I., Braye, S. and Cheng, A. (2009) *SCIE Report 28: Carers As Partners (CaPs) in Social Work Education*. London: SCIE.

Topps UK (2002) 'The National Occupational Standards for Social Work', *Skills for Care website*, http://www.skillsforcare.org.uk/developing_skills/National_Occupational_Standards/ social_work.aspx (accessed 12 March 2010).

Visser, A. (1997) 'Case based learning: Towards a computer tool for learning with cases', *New Technology in the Human Services*, 10(4): 11–13.

Waruszynski, B.T. (2002) 'Pace of technological change: Battling ethical issues in qualitative research', in W.C. van den Hoonaard (ed.), *Walking the Tightrope: Ethical Issues for Qualitative Researchers*, pp. 152–159. Toronto: Toronto University Press.

White, S., Hall, C. and Peckover, S. (2009) 'The descriptive tyranny of the Common Assessment Framework: Technologies of categorization and professional practice in child welfare', *British Journal of Social Work*, 39(7): 1197–1217.

Wilson, K., Ruch, G., Lymbery, M. and Cooper, A. (2008) *Social Work: An Introduction to Contemporary Practice*. Harlow: Pearson.

Wintour, P. (2010) 'Gordon Brown proposes personalised MyGov web services', *Guardian online*, http://www.guardian.co.uk/technology/2010/mar/22/mygov-personalised-government-web-services (accessed 22 March 2010).

Woolgar, S. (1991) 'Configuring the user: The case of usability trials', in Law, J. (ed.), *A Sociology of Monsters: Essays on Power, Technology and Domination*, pp. 57–102. London: Routledge.

Wyatt, S., Henwood, F., Hart, S. and Smith, J. (2005) 'The digital divide, health information and everyday life', *New Media & Society*, 7(2): 199–218.

Youth Justice Board (2006) 'Asset – Young Offender Assessment Profile', *Youth Justice Board website*, http://www.yjb.gov.uk/en-gb/practitioners/Assessment/Asset.htm (accessed 12 August 2009).

Youth Justice Board (2008) 'Remote Working leaflet (B384)', *Youth Justice Board website*, http://www.yjb.gov.uk/Publications/Scripts/prodView.asp?idproduct= 429&eP= (accessed 26 August 2009).

Youth Justice Board (2009) 'Tagging', *Youth Justice Board website*, http://www.yjb.gov. uk/en-gb/yjb/MediaCentre/PositionStatements/Tagging.htm (accessed 26 August 2009).

Zeman, L.D. and Swanke, J. (2008) 'Integrating social work practice and technology competencies: A case example', *Social Work Education: The International Journal*, 27(6): 601–612.

Index